GW01605754

SCHOOL WITHOUT TEARS

AN EXPERIMENT IN EDUCATION

by MOLLIE JENKINS

COLLINS

St James's Place, London

William Collins Sons & Co Ltd
London · Glasgow · Sydney · Auckland
Toronto · Johannesburg

ISBN 0 00 211676 6

First published 1973

Made and printed in Great Britain by
William Collins Sons & Co Ltd Glasgow

FOR THE PICKLEY WIZARDS

Deborah, Rebecca, Jose, Sebbie, Catherine, Nicky, Isobel, Graham, Michela, Candy, Clare, Elwyn, Edward, Antonia

Contents

CHAPTER I

Why

I wonder how many adults, looking back on their childhood days, can honestly say that they enjoyed school. I don't mean just the last few years of it, but right from the age of five, through the infant and junior years and the lower half of the secondary school, before one becomes an upper school personality with power and privileges.

Like most people I started school at five, full of pleasurable anticipation; but within weeks I had decided that this life was not for me and was desperately calculating how many more weeks, months, years it would be until I was fourteen and could 'go out to work' - glorious vision of freedom! I remember vividly the despair I felt at that endless vista of dreary imprisonment, its days filled with boredom, injustices, fear of unpredictable adults and the bullying of small boys. There were of course occasional highlights which relieved the general gloom - one or two teachers that I remember with affection and gratitude, the satisfaction of a new skill mastered, the excitement of a story that flooded the imagination with new ideas - but these were rare and memorable incidents.

The first few weeks of my school career were in fact very promising and fulfilled all my expectations. I went to school, a Roman Catholic convent, at the beginning of the summer term, just after my fifth birthday. My mother was anxious and kept assuring me that she would soon be back to take me home again, that I must be brave and not cry - assurances that were quite unnecessary as I was consumed with curiosity about life in this new place, was utterly fascinated and did not feel in the least like crying.

Three other new girls had arrived on the same day, so rather than plunge us all into the first class where the children had already begun to learn to read and write, we were to be coached in a special group by the Mother Superior herself, a wise and kindly old lady known as Mother Catherine. Our classroom was one of those functionless little rooms that seem to abound in convents, containing a bookcase full of identical leather-bound tomes with indecipherable titles, a large round mahogany table, a few straight chairs and several holy pictures on the bare walls. Unpromising as this may sound to modern educationalists, it was to us a haven of peace and pure joy. I cannot speak for my classmates, but there I experienced the pleasure and satisfaction of academic achievement every bit as intensely as in the University Library in later years.

Our routine was simple. Every morning at nine o'clock Mother Catherine took down two of the leather-bound tomes to place on each of the chairs so that we should be high enough to write comfortably at the mahogany table. Then she produced a copy for each of us of Chambers's Radiant Way First Reader, and with stubby fingers pointing the way we painfully sounded out the words letter by letter. We were fascinated by the tiny delicate pictures of children with monosyllabic names like Nell, Jess, Ann, Bob, and Bess, and by the strange words like 'gig' which meant nothing to us but conjured up a slightly unreal world. This went on until half past ten - and I never remember being tired or bored by these sessions, long though they were by modern standards. Then we were each given a pink sugar fish - I can still savour the heavenly taste of them, like peardrops - and sent out to play for ten minutes or so. We had the playground to ourselves, for our break did not coincide with that of the other children. At one end of the playground was a wooden building used for music and dancing; one day peeping in we saw a lot of little boys with paper hats and wooden swords marching up and down to music. I liked watching but had no desire to join them.

Once our sugar fish were consumed we were anxious to get back to work - obviously our classroom activities were far more interesting than chasing each other round the playground. We had been doing that sort of thing ever since we could remember and were now looking for fresh fields to conquer. The second half of the morning was devoted to writing, with a dip pen and a proper cursive script from the beginning - none of your babyish 'stick and ball' stuff. We had copybooks ruled with lines at just the right distance from each other, and you had to make your letters fit exactly into these. I can see now the intense concentration round the table as we struggled to achieve a neat page, Mother Catherine quietly encouraging our efforts but never for one moment suggesting that this was a difficult or dull task for our tender years.

It was this fact of being taken for the competent and serious human beings that we undoubtedly were that we enjoyed so much, after years of being fussed and protected as though we were incapable of serious thought or effort. Moreover our enthusiasm had so far never been dampened by fear of failure; our teacher was never angry, never ridiculed us, but was always ready to explain a thing patiently as many times as it was necessary.

The result was that we must have mastered the basic skills of reading and writing within a few weeks, though we were not in any sense a special or picked group. Two of us came from working-class, two from professional families, and none of us had any experience of reading or writing before we came to school. Nevertheless we had achieved in a particularly enjoyable and trouble-free manner, and in a few weeks at that, what most children have to spend two or three dreary years learning, by which time a lot of them have lost interest in the whole business.

Had my school life continued along these satisfactory lines all would have been well, but Mother Catherine had other things to attend to and we were now thought fit to join the rest of the five year olds in Form I. It was here that my troubles began.

The teacher in Form I was a young, softly-spoken nun called Sister Mary Therese, though I always assumed it was spelt 'Trays' and thought it affected of people to pronounce it 'Ter-ays'. The classroom was large and light and almost filled with rows of single desks. The pictures round the walls depicted the Victorian alphabet 'A is for Apple-pie, B bit it, C cut it,' and so on. On my first morning I amused myself by reading it right through, a check to my memory that Mother Catherine's teaching had been effective.

There was a large rocking horse which was a source of great delight to me, but as we were allowed to ride it only before or after school (or when we cried, but that was no good to me, I never cried in school) and competition was keen, I very rarely managed to get a turn; but the fascination of a Victorian rocking horse has remained with me to this day.

We also had a sand-tray like all 'with-it' schools in the 1930's, but this was rather an embarrassment as none of us knew what we were supposed to do with it. It was a shallow tray thinly covered with dry silver sand, but having trailed an experimental finger through it one really could not think of anything else to do with it, despite the expectant look in Sister's eye.

I remember very little in detail of what we did in that class, but what sticks in my mind is the boredom and the agony of sitting still. Upstairs with Mother Catherine I had found it no hardship to sit still for an hour and a half at a stretch as long as I had something to do, but this was different. For one thing I could never understand what was going on at the front of the classroom. Sister Therese droned on and on in her soft, rather reproachful tones, but what she wanted us to do, or what she was trying to explain, was beyond my comprehension; so I soon retired into a dream world of my own. I would surreptitiously stretch first one cramped leg and then the other under the desk, or trace pictures and letters in the dust on the desk-top until I was told to stop fidgeting; after that I would count the window-panes, first up and down and then across, and wonder whether dinner-time would ever come.

However I soon came to regard the classroom as a haven of peace and security. At playtime we were given a cup of warm milk - oh how I loathed the stuff - and released into the playground (no sugar fishes in this class). It was a good playground, with trees and seats and flowerbeds, interesting corners and hidey-holes, which should have provided five-year-olds with plenty of scope for imaginative play. To the little girls, and I suspect to some of the more sensitive or lightweight little boys, it was nightmare territory where one was exposed defenceless to the joyful sadism of the more aggressive little boys. I can still hear the pounding of feet gaining on me as I fled, followed by the pain first of hard little fists in my ribs, then of my grazed and bruised knees as I hit the ground. Worse still was when these little horrors, having felled you, sat astride your helpless form and spat on your face and stuffed your mouth with dirt and leaves.

On one occasion when I was so reduced to helplessness and misery, I spotted salvation and vengeance in the shape of Sister Therese as she emerged smiling from the door to watch her little charges playing in the sunshine. Shouting for help was out of the question, I was too busy just trying to breathe, but my mutely pleading eyes willed her to rescue me. But no! she just went on smiling sweetly, her hands serenely folded, and totally ignored my frantic SOS. My tormentors had looked up guiltily when she appeared on the scene, but seeing that they apparently had her approbation they stayed right where they were and continued with the less obvious of their tortures. At last the bell rang for our return to safety, and along with my fellow victims I complained to Sister Therese about our treatment at the hands of the bullies. She chided us gently for telling tales and assured us that the little boys were only playing! I dare say it looked that way to her, but I wonder how she herself would have coped with a man her own age intent on beating her up. I have never forgotten that nun - she still crops up in my nastier dreams, smiling like the Mona Lisa while I plead with her in vain to deliver me from unspeakable terrors.

At the age of five the idea of collective self-protection just does not occur to children, nor have they the ability to organise it. I did sometimes rather feebly try hitting back, but fighting does not come naturally to most girls and I always got the worst of the affair. Some years later, by which time I was attending the girls' department of the local Primary School, I was again in trouble from a gang of boys who lay in wait for us on the way home. By this time I knew that there was no help to be expected from the adult world, so I decided to make my own arrangements. I borrowed from home a plaited leather dog whip (which, let me say at once, we used as a lead, not as a whip) and concealed it under my coat. It gave me considerable joy to lay this across the legs of my assailants and watch them scatter in alarm. Various women who witnessed the incident protested vociferously and were all for disarming me, but encouraged by success I cracked the whip at them and ran away, and nobody volunteered to chase me. Even at that age - I must have been about eight at the time - I registered rather bitterly the fact that though 'they' (the adults) condemned my method of self-defence so roundly, none of them had come to my aid when I was attacked. I never used my whip again - I never needed to! Apparently word had got round that I was a dangerous character, and soon I did not even bother to carry it.

My schooldays took their dreary course through a misty tunnel of what I can only describe as 'unease' - a compound of sinister surroundings (dark brown echoing corridors, endless vistas of margarine-coloured walls, a frightening maze of steel bars and grilles that stretched from floor to ceiling where we hung our coats, and sickening, stinking lavatories) and a tension born of fear. The object of fear changed from the bullies of my earlier days, whom in time I had learned to cope with, to what I gradually perceived to be a far greater danger, the utterly unpredictable adult.

The behaviour that yesterday had brought forth no comment today elicited cutting scorn or a public reprimand. Apparently fortuitous circumstances, such as getting one's sums wrong instead of right, not finishing one's writing as quickly as everyone else, being unable to draw a snowdrop when the teacher could draw a perfectly good one, forgetting to change one's shoes before coming into the classroom - all these unimportant and unavoidable circumstances could bring down a whole heap of unpleasantness on one's head.

Many of the teachers, and all of the cooks, caretakers and gardeners seemed positively to dislike children; so that I was astonished one day when I was smitten with earache in school and a teacher wrapped her woollen scarf round my face and spoke gently to me. I had genuinely never suspected that these grim warders might have ordinary human concern for us like the people at home.

For a few months however the gloom lifted and I really began to enjoy school - at least as long as I was in the safety of the classroom. I was nine years old and in Form 3A, which was taken by Miss Northern, a teacher of considerable experience and rather forbidding aspect. She looked as if she wouldn't stand any nonsense, but we soon discovered that nobody felt inclined to cause trouble anyway; for one thing we were busy and interested for the first time, and above all we were happy. (Boredom must account for ninety per cent of all classroom misbehaviour.) Miss Northern - it was only much later that we even dared to think of her as Katey - was one of that rare breed that really like children, other peoples' children, which is an entirely different thing from just liking your own. I never remember her being unjust or sarcastic, or even angry, though she was firm with the lazy and the slipshod; but we were not afraid of her, and this was tremendously important. The tension was gone and we were free to enjoy learning. She introduced us to the Arthurian legends; we painted castles and knights, sighed over Lancelot and Guinevere, and wept over the Lady of Shalott. Years later I returned to them athirst for more and they remain one of my favourite corners of English literature.

She also introduced us to what we called Greek dancing - I suppose it was the fore-runner of to-day's 'music and movement' - which we did in bare feet and special short dresses the colour of autumn leaves. She made my dress for me at home one evening because my mother was ill, and I was deeply impressed by the fact that she should have taken so much trouble just for me - after all she had thirty-six of us to look after. I don't remember enjoying the dancing very much as I was far too selfconscious to respond in public even to such inviting music as this, but I liked the idea of it and certainly enjoyed listening to the music.

One scene that stands out in my memory is of a rainy day in winter when we were all returning wet and cold for afternoon school. As we came into the warm brightly-lit classroom Miss Northern was there with a towel to rub our hair dry. She made us take off our wet boots and shoes and put on our gym-shoes instead, an unusual procedure. The very fact that she was concerned about us gave me a feeling of peace and security that I had never felt in school before, and an almost tangible air of warmth and contentment spread through the classroom. Soon we were helping each other off with awkward boots, and making way round the radiators for colder newcomers; a new awareness of each other was born that grew as the term went on.

To my sorrow I was taken away from that school before I had even completed the year in 3A, and found myself at a private school again. This was a religious foundation where one might perhaps have expected to find peace and kindness. There were no aggressive males anywhere on the horizon, and only girls from 'nice' families, but I have never known any institution where loving-kindness was quite so conspicuously absent. The teachers were unpleasant in a way that only females can be to each other, with a withering contempt and dislike for the distasteful commodity known as 'girls' with which they had to deal. As always the children were infected by the attitude of the adults around them, and inflicted cruelties and miseries on each other far worse than the most aggressive males could have achieved in physical terms. Not that we children complained - we just thought that life had to be like that and accepted it. When our parents visited the school the staff were all sweetness and light and full of loving concern for us - until afterwards, when they dropped the mask with disconcerting alacrity. As long as parents are so gullible the children are completely at the mercy of the school.

My next school was a co-educational grammar school with what was known as a 'strong' headmaster, held in great esteem by parents and educational authority alike. In actual fact he was a great big bully with licence from them all to practise his sadism on a pack of helpless children. He made a practice of coming into the classroom unannounced to make sure that the teachers were doing their job properly. He would fling the door open wide and stand there glaring at us, his mean little eyes roving over us to pick out a likely victim for the morning's sport. We would stand in petrified silence gazing at the floor, waiting for the bomb to drop. After waiting for a minute or two so that we were really strung up he would fling an accusing finger at some child - preferably a nervous-looking one with glasses - and shout: 'You, what are the principal parts of fero?' Even if the wretched child did know he was usually dumb with terror, which provoked his tormentor to bellow at him louder still. In the end the child would be shaking with fright, and only then would the man be satisfied and go on to select a new victim. Fear of this man permeated the whole school; we used to tiptoe past his study where he sat like an ogre in his den, with the door open waiting to catch you. If he heard you he would roar at you to come and account for yourself, and you would be in for fifteen minutes of terrorising. I felt that there was some justice in the world when years later I heard that he had died of temper in his study - though I longed to rewrite his obituary in the local paper.

My final years were spent at a very different school, again co-educational. It was a new school, opened only a year or so before I went there, and the atmosphere was happy, friendly and relaxed. The reason was not far to find; the headmaster was a gentle kindly man, never known to beat even the toughest of his boys - and that was revolutionary in those days. The staff were for the most part young and genuinely interested in us, and there was always laughter in the air. Inevitably there was the odd battleaxe who could sometimes make life unpleasant, but the whole place was a revelation to me, a promise of a new deal for children and the proof of what could be achieved given the right people to run it. It was not just the surroundings - spacious new buildings, acres of gardens and playing-fields all round, though doubtless these helped; it was the personality of the headmaster, who commanded the love and respect of all of us because he treated each one of us kindly and reasonably, without violence or arrogance or contempt, but as a loved and respected human being. Nobody in the community remained untouched by his personality or could help reflecting it in some degree - warmth and happiness are just as contagious as fear.

It would be comforting to think that my own experiences of nearly forty years ago could not be repeated now, but I do not believe that this is so. You have only to read Caroline Glyn's 'Don't Knock the Corners Off' to realise that for some children at least things haven't changed much.

The idea of running my own school was a pipe-dream I had cherished since the age of nine or thereabouts. Not that I ever imagined I should really be able to implement it, but it was an antidote to the miseries and inadequacies of my own school life. I was a great reader of school stories, in particular Elinor Brent-Dyer's tales of the Chalet School, and what I had in mind was a small intimate community where the children had some hope of recognition as individuals, where they could live in an atmosphere of warmth and humanity. Under these conditions, I thought, school might be positively enjoyable, for there is no doubt that the company of one's contemporaries is one of the essential ingredients of an ideal childhood - given, in addition, the unobtrusive control and subtle guidance of wise and patient adults. At this stage of course the dream was entirely child-angled, with no serious thought as to how such a school could be organised, or what might be the long-term effect on its pupils. As I grew up my own experience as a pupil clarified my understanding of what were the essentials of the ideal school.

Two things must be eliminated - fear and boredom. Fear, which paralyses the mind and numbs the senses, implies boredom, for it precludes an intelligent interest in, or enjoyment of, whatever the school might be trying to teach. A child is often afraid of many things unsuspected by the adult world, but in school it boils down to three things - strange and dreary surroundings, the cruelty of other children, and the teacher. The teacher is the key to the situation because a good one can eliminate the other two fears.

There are many good teachers about, but unfortunately there are also a great many bad ones who are responsible for a lot of childhood unhappiness. There are too many teachers who do not understand children and who have no sympathy with them. They see themselves as moulders of the next generation without stopping to consider the nature of the material they are trying to mould. I am not advocating a sloppy sentimentality, which would be an equal misunderstanding of the situation, but those who handle children should at least be able to recall how they themselves thought and felt as a child, and to view the world once again in the strange and magnified way that a child sees it. It is a revealing exercise just to get down, literally, to a child's eye level and see how different the world looks from down there. People loom gigantic and menacing above you, making it easier to understand why an angry adult is so terrifying to a child - rather like being threatened by a nasty-tempered elephant. In human relationships the threat is not so much a physical one, though some teachers do still assault their pupils, and the problem of real physical violence from the child's contemporaries remains. It is rather that when the child invokes the teacher's dislike and anger, however innocently, he is liable to be persecuted, and since he is in the teacher's power to an extent that no adult is ever likely to find himself this can spell out quite a lot of misery for him.

Children are afraid of the unpredictability of adults, of unjust anger, of cold indifference, of sarcasm; they are afraid of being shouted at, and of being ridiculed. Above all they need the approbation and encouragement of the adult world - without it they are reluctant to try to learn because they are afraid of failure. Of course all this is true of us as adults too, but then we are not engulfed by the situation; we can usually escape from it, or at least view it from the outside with a sense of proportion born of a wider experience. The child is a prisoner in whatever situation he finds himself. However intolerable his life at school - or at home for that matter - he must endure it and adapt himself to it as best he can. Being extraordinarily tough creatures most children do adapt, except for the casualties who fall into the psychiatrist's hands; but everybody is searching for happiness, not just the strength to endure unhappiness.

Quite early in my childhood days I came to the conclusion that school need not be an unhappy place, given the right sort of teachers (I probably had in mind someone with the combined virtues of Saint Nicholas and the Virgin Mary). The second thing to be eliminated in my dream school was boredom, but given the 'right sort of teacher' this would present no problem. My mind envisaged a bright vista of exciting possibilities that extended to the edges of the world and beyond. Like the Pied Piper, the teacher would lead us into magic paths to explore untold delights; wherever our curiosity led us she would prove an inexhaustible guide and mentor. I was a highly imaginative child!

It was inevitable that I should become a teacher. I can't honestly say that it is the only thing that I ever wanted to do, because my real ambition was to be an opera singer, but at a more prosaic level I knew that teaching was the one thing that I could do reasonably well. I made the initial mistake of thinking that secondary school teaching would be the most interesting for me because I had enjoyed so much my own academic work. Full of enthusiasm for my subject I strode into first a private school, then a state grammar school, to teach French and Latin to girls aged from eleven to nineteen. Unfortunately, despite my best efforts I could bring very few of my pupils to share my enthusiasm, and the savage indifference of the younger generation to the beauties of the French language almost drove me to despair.

I liked the children at the private school well enough – they were a happy uninhibited lot who had never had much cause to be afraid of the adult world. My second school, the state grammar school, was a different matter. It was an old-fashioned girls' school with a dangerously incompetent headmistress, and though some of the staff were good and devoted teachers, unhappiness sat on the place like a fog, seeping into all its corners. The children exhibited all the symptoms of boredom and despondency that I knew so well from my own childhood, ranging from sullen non-co-operation to active delinquency. I felt helpless to fight against the atmosphere - the only hope would have been to open all the windows, sack the headmistress, and start again. Eventually this was what happened, but it took years of hard work on the part of the staff and a new generation of children to put things right.

Meanwhile I came to the conclusion that secondary school teaching would never satisfy me because one never got to know the children well enough. Teaching only French, I moved from class to class and saw each group of children only three or four times a week; at this rate it would take too long to build up the personal relationships which I believe are essential to good teaching.

My third school was another private school where I taught rather younger children, including boys this time. There was more chance to get to know the children but the place still left me dissatisfied. The staff were human and friendly, some of them were good teachers, and the children were not unhappy, but it saddened me to think of what could have been done there and was not being done because the place was just a commercial venture with no real interest in the children as people. I found myself calculating what the income of the place must be and what could be done with it in terms of equipment, books, and just sheer fun for the children.

Eventually my disillusionment acquired a new edge when it came to finding a school for our own children. We lived in a house in the middle of the town with no garden and no other children living nearby, and current trends in education dictated that they should go to a nursery school. The local authority ran only six such schools, and as all of these had a long waiting list a private school was indicated. Knowing very little about such places I visited practically every nursery school in the area, but I was depressed by what I saw.

The first one was presided over by a horsy lady with a voice like a sergeant-major who assured us jocularly that she never had any trouble with new children - she just walloped them if they misbehaved. The truth of this statement was born out years later by two of her ex-pupils, who told me that from the age of three they had been thumped and slapped by the horsy lady and her minions. We hastily withdrew from that place and went to see the one down the road.

Here the proprietress seemed to know very little about the nursery, being much more interested in the higher reaches of the school, but she obligingly introduced us to a charming girl of about eighteen who was apparently in sole charge. It turned out that she was not trained in nursery work, nor indeed in teaching or child care of any sort, but she liked little children - fair enough! She could still be an excellent teacher. Unfortunately she had to cope with twenty-five children in what was virtually an empty room, as the owner of the school evidently regarded the nursery as a good money-spinner and saw no need to spend the precious fees on equipment for the children. When we were there the children were fighting with rulers, borrowed from an older class with the idea of teaching the little ones to draw straight lines with them. The teacher remonstrated mildly with them but she had long ago lost any control over her charges.

We moved on to the next place on the list. This had the

advantage of having a properly qualified nursery teacher in charge, but like the others she had to live, and had taken in far more children than she could really cope with. Our impression was of tiny overcrowded rooms presided over by people of doubtful suitability for the job; dirty walls and battered toys. There was quite a lot of good equipment here, but not enough to go round; we noticed that the largest and most aggressive little boys monopolised the best toys and the others never got a look in. I thought it was a pretty miserable place from the child's point of view.

There was another nursery school, said to be very good, with a Froebel-trained staff, but needless to say it had a long waiting list and we had only recently come to the town.

In the end I joined up with three friends and we took it in turns to have all the children to play, so that most days they had companions of their own age and we had some time to ourselves. In the afternoons, apart from taking them out, I taught my own children to read. I did this partly because I enjoyed it so much; partly because I felt that this particular job was my privilege and no one else's; and partly because I wanted to make sure that they learned quickly and painlessly an accomplishment so essential to a child's happiness in the present day.

The problem loomed up again some years later when our third child was born, a girl this time. By now I was thoroughly interested in nursery and primary education and had some years of reading and discussion behind me. I was absolutely convinced of the value of a good nursery school and knew just what I wanted for our own child. But where to find it? By the time she was two years old and her sister well on the way my mind was made up. I would run my own nursery school.

CHAPTER 2

How

No one can just decide to start a school and go straight into business - there is a whole lot of red tape to be negotiated first, which is perhaps just as well for the prospective customers. Nursery schools come under the aegis of the superintendent Health Visitor, who called on me to inspect the premises and acquaint me with the regulations. She greeted my enthusiasm for the venture with sardonic amusement, implying that I had no idea of what I was letting myself in for. Nor had I, as it turned out!

She measured the cubic air space and informed me that I would be allowed to take up to ten children, including my own two, providing I had a full-time assistant, three pots and one lavatory - though the implication that one might want to pot half the establishment simultaneously showed a lack of practical experience on the part of the local authority, who presumably framed this unrealistic law. I must also provide ten coat pegs at least six inches apart, ten more pegs with a separate towel for each child, and enough toys to keep ten children amused. In addition I must keep a register available for inspection at any time, and inform the local authority of all outbreaks of dysentery and vermin. She left me with fervent good wishes and a pile of catalogues from Nursery School suppliers.

The catalogues were tremendous fun and I spent many happy hours making lists of equipment to buy or make. I was determined that the children should have more than enough of everything that they needed, a fascinating array to tempt even the dullest and most unadventurous. To this end I borrowed £200 from my father, vaguely hoping that one day I should be able to repay it.

First we needed good strong child-sized tables that would take any amount of ill-treatment - a criterion that went for all our equipment. Everything had to stand the test of being jumped on, overturned, thrown, scratched, bitten, and painted by healthy five-year-olds. A Norwich firm made me some beautiful beech tables, formica-topped in red with a pattern of gold stardust, and ten sturdy beech chairs which, like the tables, could be stacked. The tables could also be fitted together in groups. They served us well - even after six years of hard usage they were as good as new.

I was lucky enough to buy a few things second hand - a long cloakroom bench with accommodation for shoes underneath; two double-sided easels, child-sized, with boards attached for chalk or painting, fitted with troughs to hold paint-pots; a few percussion instruments; one or two extra chairs and folding tables.

The help was enlisted of a boy who was learning carpentry at the Technical College and together we made stands to take the stipulated number of coat and towel pegs, and, our *chef d'œuvre*, a Wendy House. This consisted of a hinged frame hung with 4 ft × 4 ft hardboard panels; it had no roof, but as the walls came well above the children's heads they never missed it, and it was lighter that way. One panel had a door, painted bright red and sporting a brass doorknob and a gay brass knocker. The centre panel had a window cut out, with curtains to draw for privacy, and a red shelf which fitted across the sill when the house was serving as a shop or a puppet theatre. The children helped to paint the walls with several coats of emulsion paint, an activity which delighted them and which was repeated many times during its active life.

A carpenter made me two sturdy long low bookcases. In the early days these were used for displaying toys; bookcases as such are of little use to small children since the spines of large picture books are rarely their most interesting aspect. Instead I made a bookrack by tacking pegboard on to a three-sided clothes-horse and fitting it on both sides with ledges and wires to display the books *en face*. This had the advantage of creating a secluded little bay in the corner of the room; one or two child-sized armchairs with gay cushions and a table completed the book corner, where children liked to hide away to enjoy their books in peace.

One big disadvantage was that, as I have said, we had no proper garden. We had some space, a concreted walled yard, which got plenty of sun, and was safe in that the children could not wander out on to the road. There was however enough space for a swing, a sandpit, a little square with some benches, and a broad path adequate for the circulation of several wheeled vehicles at a time. The rather battered grey walls looked much more cheerful when treated to a coat of cream paint, and I planted flowers in boxes and tubs; two old sycamores overhung the walls.

The sandpit was about four feet square, with a concrete base surrounded by a wall of foot-high concrete blocks, which in turn were surmounted by oak seating which ran all the way round. This helped to keep the sand clean and in one place, and the children could sit all the way round the edge to play instead of lumbering about in the middle and treading on each other's castles or whatever.

Nearby was an outside tap, with a removable key so that it could be immobilised when necessary. An old baby-bath on a stand, a plastic paddling pool, and a supply of plastic buckets, bowls, jars, cups, bottles, funnels, tubing, sieves, and an old egg-whisk completed our basic equipment for water-play.

A storeroom led out on to the yard and here we kept an assortment of toys to be brought out a few at a time - two slides, one a real baby slide, the other higher and less protected for the more adventurous; a rocking-boat; two or three tricycles and scooters and a red pedal car; wheelbarrows, hobby-horses, stilts; things to push, like horses on wheels, carts, and a stout wooden pram; a hefty home-made train with lots of wagons; hoops, ropes, large balls and bean-bags; tough wooden boxes and large wooden bricks; but brightest and best of all was a huge red engine with a silver bell, big enough to get right inside and drive, the sort usually only to be found in fairgrounds.

Some of this assortment were bought new, some second-hand and repainted, some were home-made. The main thing was that there was plenty to keep ten children occupied for some time to come. At a later date we replaced the swing by a tubular steel climbing frame which consisted of two towers connected by an overhead ladder and a scrambling net; from this we suspended a rope ladder, a trapeze, a knotted rope, and a monkey-swing - the latter was known as 'the lid' because it was just that, a large tin lid with a rope through the middle; the object is to sit on the lid and hang on to the rope, but it isn't as easy as it sounds.

There was more room inside the house. To begin with the main nursery was a square, carpeted room on the first floor; here were the tables and chairs, the book corner, the shelves of toys. The fireplace was boarded up with hardboard painted over with blackboard paint; a tin of coloured chalk beside it provided endless joy. The walls were painted the colour of sunshine and decorated with pictures; it was a cheerful peaceful place.

Opposite this room was our family drawing-room, some twenty-four feet long by fifteen, with a big bay window looking out on to the busy High Street. The window seat was a favourite grandstand for watching the world go by. We pushed the furniture back to the walls and used it for a general stamping-ground in the mornings. It possessed a piano, a television set, and a record-player; we also kept our percussion instruments there. Its other asset was a vast deep sofa which was ideal for story-book sessions; if I sat in the middle there was room for all the children around and above me, and everyone could see the pictures.

On the ground floor was a room which housed the Wendy House and all its furniture - dolls and their beds, pots, pans, cooker, dresser; tables and chairs, cups and plates, and anything else that fertile imaginations could think up. There was also material for shop play; one most prized possession was a large box of life-sized plastic fruit from Woolworths, and a length of sham 'grass' begged from a local greengrocer. Baskets of conkers, cannisters of beans, jars of shells, all added variety, with an old set of kitchen scales, one or two scoops, and a supply of paper bags.

Down there too we kept a hamper of dressing-up clothes - old curtains and night-dresses, scarves and hats and belts of all sorts, artificial flowers and ribbons and bits of lace. I made good strong bus conductor's and postman's hats which stood up to years of wear - these were both popular roles. We had a postbox and a hessian mailbag, and a ticket-machine with rolls of tickets which I bought by the gross. Hospitals was another favourite game. An old sheet made several white coats, aprons, nurses' and doctors' caps and surgical masks. One or two strong plastic stethoscopes, a few crêpe bandages, and a limitless supply of 'sticking-plasters' (Stick-on plastic cut up into suitable sizes, so that the backing could be peeled off most realistically) completed the props for this game.

We had one more room, next door to the main nursery. This was known as the 'Workroom' because it held a large old wooden kitchen table and an assortment of tools - small hacksaws, small pincers and pliers and hammers, a mallet, and tins of one-inch panel pins. Boxes under the table held oddments of wood, and one or two strong wooden boxes did duty as saw-horses. The room also held big cupboards right along one wall where we kept stocks of paper and paint, Plasticine and clay, and all the toys we had no room for in the nursery.

My second daughter was born in November, and I spent that winter stitching and hammering and painting in readiness for the opening of the school after Easter. I wanted everything to be new and light and cheerful, warm and safe as a Victorian nursery - in fact as different from the dismal schools of my own childhood as possible.

I had decided to accept children from the age of two and a half because this was the age of my own elder daughter at the time. Experience showed that this was really too young and later I changed the minimum age to three; even then the younger children only came for an hour or two on two or three mornings a week. The state nurseries at that time were insisting that even three year olds should stay for the whole day and this was obviously wrong for both mother and child.

Because I was particularly concerned to soften the impact of the outside world on children who would be venturing beyond the security of their family and home for the first time, I decided that mothers should be free to come and go as they pleased throughout all our activities, and that the children should only come for as long as they wanted to. I counted on the attractions of the school gradually weaning the child from his utter dependence on mother and home, but at his own pace. This is in fact what happened in most cases, though some of the mothers were so anxious to escape from their children that they would not have the patience to wean them gently. This sometimes resulted in panic and increasing resistance on the part of the child. When this happened their fear of being abandoned outweighed any attractions the school could offer, and created the very unhappiness that I was so anxious to avoid. In these cases I tried to persuade the parents either to stay with the child at school, or to take him home again until he volunteered to come of his own free will.

It is true that I could hold a screaming struggling child by superior physical force while the mother made her escape, and comfort the unhappy child afterwards as best I could. Even worse was when the mother, trying to soften the blow, promised to return in a few minutes when in fact she had no intention of doing so. This is a cruel and useless device - it adds to the child's misery when he realises that he has been tricked and, much worse, causes him to doubt his mother's love for him, if she is prepared to lie to him in order to escape from him. Children, though inarticulate sometimes, are not stupid, especially when it comes to anything as important to them as personal relationships. In such cases I did usually manage to calm down the child when he realised that his mother really had gone and was not coming back for some hours. A casual observer could have been forgiven for supposing that the policy of 'firmness for the child's - or mother's? - own good' was justified. In fact such children were restless and unhappy; they could not settle down to enjoy school, and often were to be seen prowling anxiously round the gate like lost souls waiting for their mother's return. The problem usually resolved itself in time, but only after a lot of unnecessary misery; and in some cases such children failed to overcome their anxiety and carried their restlessness with them on to the primary school, never really settling down to enjoy themselves. On the other hand those children whose mothers took the time and patience to help them adjust to the wider world of school not only enjoyed life to the full but generally turned out much more stable and happy people later on.

Although I had no intention of running a day nursery various people seemed to think that I should be persuaded to do so, and I was saddened by the number of young women who came to me at that time to try and persuade me to look after their babies for them. I am not speaking now either of the people who were in dire economic necessity and therefore had to go out to work, nor of the people who were just looking for a good nursery school for a few hours a day; these people just wanted to get rid of their children for as long as possible, and one wonders why they bothered to have them at all since they apparently get so little pleasure from them. They were all women who wanted to 'be themselves', to go back to the work which they thought was so much more important than their own babies. They ranged from the feckless young mother to the arrogant female intellectual, and they brought me babies from a few months old upwards. They were not usually interested in how I proposed to care for their children - they just wanted to be rid of them.

When I thought it was any use I tried gently to convince these women that what their babies needed was them and their love; nothing that I or anyone else could do could compensate a child for the loss of his mother's love. No nursery nurse or temporary mother's help can possibly give the intimate love of a mother. In a group there are other children to be looked after, and a baby demands all of its mother's attention for just a little time in its life. No nanny dare give the child the love he craves - if she did she could not bear the pain of parting with him, or of not having complete possession of him.

Later on, because of my earlier experiences, I never accepted any child under the age of three, and then only on condition that the mother promised to accept my ruling on the acclimatisation process. I can call to mind two particular children whose mothers fall into the 'arrogant intellectual' class. Both these women pestered me to take their children, quoting the importance of their own jobs as an inducement to make an exception of my usual rule in their case. I refused not only because I thought the children were too young, but also because I knew that I could not possibly give them all the love and attention that they lacked at home. The best thing for them would have been a permanent and devoted nanny, but unfortunately nursery schools were cheaper. I have followed both these children with interest through their subsequent school careers. Both are very intelligent, but unhappy, and a great problem to their respective schools. Despite their intelligence they make little progress with their work - they seem incapable of concentrating. They are unpopular with the other children - inevitably, because of their failure to make normal personal relationships - and they stretch the patience of their teachers to breaking point by their determined non-co-operation.

There was a great shortage of nursery schools at that time

and the idea of do-it-yourself playgroups had hardly been born. When I first announced my intention of starting such a group around my own children the idea was greeted with enthusiasm by all my friends and acquaintances with small children; so it was with some surprise that I realised that I was going to be hard put to it to find enough children to start. Ruefully I had to accept the fact that however much my friends might applaud my enterprise they were not going to be the first to trust their children to the new venture; they wanted to stand back and see how it worked out first. By the middle of the first term I had a waiting list, and soon could have filled the available places several times over, but I was always grateful to the handful of parents who backed me right at the beginning.

At last all was ready. The nursery looked most inviting with its fresh paint and its abundance of bright new toys and picture books. Ten empty coatpegs, each bearing a picture by which its owner could identify it, matched by ten pegs bearing dwarf-sized striped towels, and ten mugs for the mid-morning milk, all decorated with the same set of pictures, stood waiting for their first ten owners.

The law stipulated that I must have an assistant, so I had arranged with five of the mothers to come and help one morning a week each; these only paid half fees, two pounds ten a term instead of five pounds. I had good domestic help at that time which meant that I was free to devote all my attention to the children. We were to operate mornings only, from nine to twelve, Mondays to Fridays.

That first morning remains vividly in my memory. By nine o'clock all the children had arrived and were taking in their surroundings with bright eyes. About five of their mothers had decided to stay too, which made the nursery somewhat overcrowded. Soon the atmosphere began to thaw and the children got more adventurous; they wanted to see and examine everything, and began to pull first one thing then another off the shelves. Jigsaw puzzles and various fitting-toys went flying, books were flung round the room. The less inhibited shouted with excitement and the nervous watched the mounting chaos with alarm. The mothers all started talking at once, flinging conflicting advice and instructions in all directions; I tried vainly to assert my authority but could not be heard above the din. Then one rowdy little boy snatched a pot of beads from the shelf and threw it up in the air with a joyous 'whoopee!' He followed it up with boxes of bricks, jigsaw puzzles, and anything else that came to hand, until the floor was covered with débris and we had all collapsed in helpless laughter. At this point we decided that this might be the moment to take a mid-morning break, so we all trooped downstairs for milk and biscuits and to play outside. This kept them all harmlessly absorbed for some time, so I thought it might be safe to leave the Mums in charge while I sneaked off upstairs to feed my younger daughter, then aged about six months. A few minutes later I heard the ominous sound of breaking glass and rushed down to find that young Jimmy had put the hobby-horse through the dining-room window. Moreover the yard was awash and several of the children soaked through as a result of some uninhibited water-play. I dried off the victims as best I could and dressed them in clothes from the family wardrobe - to which they objected most vigorously - then tried to restore order by settling everyone down for a story. This was almost a success, except that the children whose mothers were present would keep up a whispered commentary to their parents which completely distracted the rest of the group.

By the end of that first morning I was completely exhausted and sat down to do some hard thinking.

It was evident that some rules were called for if ever I was to establish any sort of order; and order, I felt, was necessary if the children were to feel happy and secure. I must collect the children under my own authority. This was almost impossible as long as their mothers were there giving contrary instructions, but it went against my whole policy to banish the mothers - they were an essential part of the scene. It was no problem later on when we were already established as a group, but at that point we were all new together and the group had yet to be welded from those most unclubbable members of society, very young children. Firstly then I must persuade the mothers to adopt a passive role, just to sit there quietly in the background, joining in a child's activity only when asked, taking their cue from me.

Secondly we must have a few rules about the toys. It was important that all the toys should be accessible to the children so that they could see all the possibilities and choose what interested them. Toys hidden away in a cupboard cannot stimulate anyone to new ideas and possibilities. On the other hand they must learn to take care of them or there would soon be no toys left. It seems to me a negative policy just to clear up after children all the time - unnecessary too, because they are quite capable of clearing up after themselves if taught to do so. So I stipulated that everybody could choose whatever he liked from the shelf, but after he had finished playing with it he must put it back as he found it, with all its parts in order, before taking another one; and he could only have one toy at a time. If he chose to throw a jar of beads all over the floor that was his affair, but he had to pick them all up again before he could have anything else to play with. (If of course he spilled them by accident we were all most sympathetic and helped him to pick them up again, but that was different.)

It took quite a lot of time and patience to establish this rule in the beginning, but then everyone accepted it, newcomers included. Remembering how afraid I had been as a child of angry adults, particularly outside the home, my policy was endless patience but firm insistence, on the water and stone principle. I concentrated on instilling just one thing at a time; when this rule had become second nature to everyone I then worked to persuade the children to complete whatever task they had set themselves, whether it was a jigsaw puzzle (unless they had chosen one that was obviously too difficult for them) or a picture or a Plasticine model. Some children will restlessly take one toy after another and never settle to anything. This is fair enough when they are new and want to explore all the possibilities at once, but it can become a habit and then they never experience the satisfaction of accomplishment or learn to concentrate on anything for any length of time. This training soon bore fruit; in a short time the nursery presented a peaceful scene each morning with all the children quietly absorbed in their own affairs, some of them singing contentedly to themselves the while.

The third need in those early days was to establish a routine so that the children knew what happened next. In fact the morning soon developed its own pattern, which was as follows.

As the children arrived they came up to the nursery and made for their favourite toy. Some of them liked always to have a particular seat; if so I always reserved it for them. It seemed to me important that they should feel at home there, that they should be able to claim territorial rights if they wanted to. I greeted each child and tried to talk to each one alone for a few minutes; I did not get much response at first from the shy ones - it was weeks before some of them talked to me spontaneously - but I felt we were really getting somewhere when they did. This question of communication is a vital one in the development of both the individual and the group. Some children of course are naturally friendly and will chatter away charmingly from the moment they meet you. Others find communication a real stumbling block, through shyness or fear, there are many different reasons, but it is one that must be overcome if the child is to be happy among his fellows. So we talked a lot in our group - quietly, naturally, and whenever we felt like it. I discouraged the noisy show-off - there is always one in every group - and they too soon got the idea and joined in the conversation quite sensibly. Gradually the shy ones would join in, and eventually they too would come bouncing in in the morning eager to tell their latest news.

For the best part of the next forty minutes the children would be absorbed in their toys. The collection on the shelves was not quite as random as the casual observer might have supposed. It included apparatus to train the hands to manipulate small pieces more and more accurately, the eye to judge size and to recognise shapes, to match colours. Each toy set the child a task which helped him to recognise the laws inherent in the concrete world around him, and gave him practice in sorting, grading, classifying its materials. In this very early stage the jigsaw puzzles, for instance, were very simple - a large clear picture, with objects cut out so that they could be lifted out by means of a projecting pin and stood up on the table. But recognising that the shape of the dog fitted the dog-shaped hole left in the puzzle and not the boy-shaped hole is an early stage in the process which leads later to recognising the difference in shape between the letters c and o, or h and b. The Kiddiecraft Posting Box and the wooden house served the same purpose - both have holes cut in the lid in geometric shapes and corresponding solid shapes to post through them.

The screw toys (a wooden car, an engine, a roundabout, which can be taken apart and put together again by means of a hefty wooden screwdriver) not only develop manual skill and dexterity, but also train the memory and focus attention on the construction of the toy. The child must manipulate screws and screwdriver, hold two parts together with one hand while he fixes them with the other; and having dismantled the thing must remember how it fits together again. This knowledge he puts to good use when playing with the Giant Matador, a useful and popular constructional toy consisting of solid wooden wheels, blocks and slabs with holes in them, which are connected with large dowels and bolts.

Beads are always a great nursery favourite. We had all sorts: plastic 'poppit' necklaces from Woolworths, big round wooden ones, square, oval, bell-shaped, all colours and sizes; tiny glass ones (harmless if swallowed) - hundreds of them to run through the hands and to thread on to plastic-covered wire. We had coloured laces (like boot-laces, with a metal tag at one end and a knot at the other) to thread the wooden ones, and the children were allowed to go home proudly in the necklaces they had made as long as they brought them back the next day, which they nearly always did. They soon progressed from random arrangements of the beads to sorting colours, shapes and sizes, and then to working out quite complicated patterns - six red, three white, two blue, and so on - long before they had officially learned to count.

Other toys teach the child to notice difference in size and

to sort the pieces out in progressive order; the Kiddiecraft pyramid and the Escor clown, which consists of a series of wooden discs of increasing diameter to slip on to a wooden dowel; and the traditional Russian dolls which fit one inside the other.

One of our favourite toys was a wooden shoe with lace-holes and a real lace to thread through them - excellent practice for the children in learning to cope with their own shoes. But the chief joy lay in the wooden figures of the Old Woman and her children, five blue boys and five red girls. These could be popped into the shoe through a hole near the top, but could only be got out again by unlacing the whole shoe - and if you wanted to fasten them in again you just had to learn to lace up the shoe. All the children learned to count up to ten in no time at all, just making sure that the Old Woman's family was complete. They learned incidently that there are five twos and two fives in ten, and that eleven is an odd number because the Old Woman did not have a partner, and so on.

As the children played with these toys, at the tables or sitting on the floor, my assistant and I sat among them and gave help when asked (though the help never added up to doing the job for the child) or just admired and offered helpful suggestions. There was usually a gentle hum of chatter, every now and then breaking off into community singing or chanting nursery rhymes or finger plays. For the uninitiated, finger plays are rhymes accompanied by miming with the hands; everyone must have done 'Fly away Peter, fly away Paul' as a small child, or 'Here's a church and here's a steeple', but nursery teachers acquire a vast repertoire of them. For some reason small children enjoy performing these finger plays enormously, and they serve the additional purpose of exercising the fingers (thus making them more supple and deft at manipulating the screws and beads and little bits of jigsaw puzzle) and of socialising the child. At this age (2 to 3 years) the idea of doing anything with other people is a fairly revolutionary one.

As well as the toys there were always books displayed temptingly on the bookrack. There was a collection of picture books with good clear pictures on a variety of topics including a few ABC books. From the beginning the children were taught to handle books reverently, to open them on a flat surface and to put them back in the rack properly afterwards, and I rarely found it necessary to restrict access to them. Deliberate tearing or scribbling in books was greatly frowned upon; the occasional offender was treated to surprised reproach: 'I thought you were old enough for proper books!' and regretfully confined to 'baby' books for a day or two, the rag or cardboard variety.

Also readily available was an inexhaustible supply of paper and a variety of drawing implements. We had big wax crayons (the little ones are too fiddling for small hands to grasp properly), fibre-tip pens - these were very popular - ordinary Biros for those who wanted to be like Daddy, and specially thick lead pencils custom-made for small hands. There was also coloured chalk, for use both on the big blackboard and on small home-made blackboards, and on sugar-paper. We stocked four kinds of paper for drawing and painting: plain white kitchen paper in sheets of 20 in × 30 in downwards, and even larger sheets of sugar paper which came in black, grey, and half a dozen colours. By 'downwards' I mean that apart from the big sheets, the paper was offered in many different shapes and sizes - circles, ovals, rectangles, hexagons, and so on, each referred to by its proper geometrical name as these are as easy to learn as any other and one might as well be accurate. We also had brown paper and newspaper which tended to be used for large-scale work - as on the day that Jimmy had a great urge to paint a mural; it was a nice day so I sellotaped large sheets of newspaper together right across one wall of the yard; he spent a blissful morning executing his *chef d'œuvre* in green, pink and purple. Unfortunately he decided to set the picture off with a frame of purple stripes, which remained on the cream-painted wall long after he had carried his masterpiece lovingly home.

Every young child is fascinated by the effect of a writing implement on paper; once he has discovered it he needs no encouragement to go on experimenting with lines and colours and shapes, while incidentally learning the complicated co-ordination of eye and muscle necessary to control it. By the time he comes to learn to write he progresses naturally to the much more precise and controlled shapes and patterns demanded, whereas the child who has hardly held a pencil before coming to school at five has no control over his hand and finds writing a difficult and lengthy process.

In the workroom next to the nursery were the two easels with sheets of paper pinned to either side, and jars of ready-mixed powder paint each with its own large brush. The colours were always mixed thick and bright - if you are mean with powder paint you simply get anaemic looking stuff about as exciting as dish-water. So I always kept a large assortment of colours ready-mixed, an irresistible galaxy of pinks and yellows, orange and peacock blues, white and black, every shade I could think of, but all bright and opaque. The children were swathed in huge rubber overalls and their sleeves rolled above the elbow before thcy were allowed to savour the delicious moment of the first stroke of colour on the virgin paper. Of course most of them got in a terrible mess at first, with rivers of paint flowing in all directions, but everything was washable - certainly the floor and the aprons and their hands - and the paint was necessarily the sort that would easily wash out of clothes. Before long they learned the knack of wiping the laden brush across the top of the jar so that they did not get too much paint on the paper, of washing the brush in clean water when it got mixed up with other colours, so that the paint in each jar remained bright and unadulterated. Rolls of kitchen paper towels were kept handy for mopping up when the paint got out of control, but in a surprisingly short time most of the children could safely be left in the workroom with only occasional supervision from the next room.

For about three quarters of an hour then from the time they arrived, the children would be fairly quiet, playing with toys, looking at books, painting or drawing, and chatting quietly. Sometimes someone would be feeling restless and in this case he could play outside by himself (I could keep an eye on him through the window). If there were several restless souls the assisting mother would take them downstairs to the playroom to play with the Wendy House. It did not often happen for some reason - perhaps they were afraid of missing something if they left the group even for a short time. It was one of the disadvantages of the way that our available space was arranged that all the possible activities could not be supervised at the same time. On the other hand it meant that noisy play downstairs could not be heard from the nursery, and I came to believe very firmly in the importance of maintaining an atmosphere of quiet and calm at the heart of things - given the space and freedom for any amount of noise and letting off steam on the periphery. I think some children do not get enough time to be quiet and to concentrate for any length of time on what interests them.

Too often they are constantly interrupted by over-energetic siblings, and even at some nursery schools there is a continual racket and jostling that would drive most adults mad.

When I noticed that the children had had enough of sitting down and playing, we would put everything away and repair to the big drawing-room across the landing for our daily music session. When the children were very young this consisted of free dancing to music played on records or on the piano, and freestyle accompaniment with a variety of percussion instruments. I used all types of music, from classical to jazz, Sousa marches, Strauss waltzes, and the latest instrumental pop records. It was to these last that the children responded most vigorously - the current ones included 'Nautilus', a nice bubbly concoction to which they glided in sinister fashion being fish and submarines; 'Telstar', evocative of awe-inspiring planets twirling in space, which they specially loved, and on its flip side a jungle piece which inspired them to slink or creep or prowl or stalk round an imaginary tropical forest in various guises. At that time the 'Twist' was all the rage and even the very young could execute its fast swirling motion with considerable skill. Some children seem to have a perfect sense of rhythm even as young as a year old - probably those who come from homes where they hear a lot of music from the beginning. I have certainly seen children too young to walk sitting on the floor and jigging in perfect time and with obvious enjoyment to music. Others seem unable to discern the beat even at the age of five or six, though I have never had a child who did not pick it up eventually through school music sessions. With these small children I found the jazz records with their strong beat just what was needed to get even the most unmusical feet tapping. We clapped and marched and banged drums in time to the music, and there was no doubt that being able to dance in time to the tune increased enormously the child's pleasure in the music.

We also learned lots of 'action songs', where the children mime the words of the song; these were always popular. I noticed that one or two very shy children who talked very little in the early days (including one who had quite a bad stammer) always joined in the singing and the nursery rhymes as confidently as anyone else. To see what would happen I introduced some singing games where one or more children have to sing or say solo lines. The extroverts always clamoured for these parts, and I let them perform for a little while until everyone must be sure of the words; then I suggested that perhaps some of the other children would like a turn, and eventually even our stammerer was claiming his rights and taking a turn at the solo part without difficulty or embarrassment.

After the music session we went downstairs for milk and biscuits and to play outside or in the playroom. Everyone helped himself to one or two biscuits out of the tin, cries of indignation greeting the miscreant who took three or four. Though most of the children were under three years old at that time they all had a very clear understanding of the numbers up to four. Of course we counted everything on every possible occasion, so that everyone could count up to ten, but counting is not the same as really understanding what the numbers mean. So the children were given continual experience of number: 'Get mugs for yourself and Peter and Sally, how many will that be?' 'How many children are playing in the sandpit? There is room for four, is there room for you?' 'Are there enough chairs for these three children?' and so on. At this stage it was a case of language; later on we learned to write and recognise the symbol and name for each number. If you think this is easy, just try making up an arbitary symbol and name for each number and try counting that way (without looking at your key) and you will have more sympathy with the small child who has to learn so much that is new to him.

At that stage we had not persuaded the local authority to let us have free milk, so the milk was poured straight from large bottles into the children's mugs. They asked for what they wanted - a lot or a little, a quarter, three quarters, a whole mugful - and then fell to comparing the varying amount in their mugs. Unconsciously they were acquiring mathematical terms and concepts which would be built into their understanding when they came to use them later on. My job was to guide them to an awareness of the world around them and teach them the words they needed to talk about it; the rest they would do for themselves.

For the next hour the children played outside or in the playroom on the ground floor whose windows gave on to the yard, so that I could keep an eye on both places at once. The first half of that first term happened to be unusually wet and the playroom was used to capacity. After half-term the sun came out and we transferred practically all our activities outside - even the music, for which we ran the record player by means of a flex through the window.

It was during these free play sessions, when the children were no longer under close supervision, that I kept a particularly sharp eye open for bullying. Not that I believe that children of two or three years old deliberately set out to be nasty to other children in a sadistic sense. They are however devoid of any finer feelings in their relationship with other people, and animal-like in their egocentricity. They will pursue the particular toy that they want with a single-mindedness that precludes any social niceties, and if they are frustrated by another child will hit out (if they happen to be the aggressive sort) or wail loudly. Some children are too afraid to enter into the scrum for what they want, and hang about rather miserably watching with covetous eyes the enjoyment of their braver companions. The more philosophical ones content themselves with the toys that nobody else wants - until some other child sees them enjoying themselves and promptly relieves them of their spoil. This situation is often left to take its course, the adults following a policy of non-interference. The law of the jungle operates, the law of natural selection; the aggressive ones have everything their own way, the weaker ones either learn to accept an inferior position in the scheme of things, or they learn to get what they want by low cunning.

My own childhood memories convince me that adults should and must interfere to protect little children from each other, just as they protect them from all other natural dangers. Though the dangers here may not be so obvious to the unimaginative parent or teacher, they are real enough to the child. School is the child's first contact with the outside world, where other people's interests conflict with his. At home wise parents arrange his life to avoid open conflict, but his school-mates have no such consideration for him. Moreover it is at this early age that his character is being formed, and is therefore most susceptible to damage.

Take the case of three children who all want the same tricycle. Peter simply grabs it, and when Jonathan tries to take it from him he hits or pushes Jonathan as hard as he thinks necessary to deter him. If Jonathan yells Peter is interested at the effect he has caused and will probably hit him again to see whether it evokes the same reaction. At the age of two or three he doesn't realise that his actions cause Jonathan pain or fear or anger - this feat of imagination comes much later. All he knows is that when he hits or pushes Jonathan, Jonathan makes a funny noise. If Jonathan happens to be equally aggressive he will hit back and a fight will develop, but the end result will be that one child will have discovered that he can get what he wants by aggression, and the other that if he tries to take what he wants he gets hurt, and will therefore think twice before competing again. He may eventually give up even trying, but still be resentful and jealous of Peter. Richard wants the tricycle too, but after watching the fight between Peter and Jonathan he may be too afraid even to touch the tricycle, in case Peter comes and hits him. Thus all three children are developing attitudes that will hamper their adjustment to society. Eventually they will have to conform to the accepted code of adult civilised behaviour, but meanwhile they may have become unpopular bullies, or be crippled by nervousness and unable to enjoy the company of their contemporaries, or be so convinced of their own inferiority that they will never put any effort into anything and so fulfill their own expectation of failure. This may sound melodramatic when discussing a group of three-year-olds playing, but you have only to get to know a class of prep-school boys or upper primary school children to realise that these things happen.

Of course the world is not perfect and children must learn to cope with bullying, but they can learn this better later as they gradually impose their own group discipline. This is in fact what happens, and they need less and less the help and protection of adults, though they always need a final court of appeal. I have no patience with the parents and teachers who ban what they choose to call 'tale-bearing'; they would use a different name for their own demands for justice if they themselves were assaulted or robbed. We have no right to expose children to an anarchy that we ourselves would not dare to live with. In proportion to their inability to protect themselves they have a right to protection from the adults who have thrown them into this situation, to give them time to develop their own sense of law and justice as well as their own self-confidence.

Not that it is any good getting angry with the aggressive children or over-sympathetic with the frightened ones. It is simply a case of instilling acceptable social behaviour. The children have to learn and then to accept the system of taking turns with the popular toys, to learn that aggressive behaviour does not bring them what they want; (if, for instance, they are relegated to the back of the queue every time they invoke the priority of might over right).

It is more difficult to deal with the child who loses his temper and makes a really vicious attack on another child, such as biting him or whacking him over the head with a spade. Until his rage has abated it is useless to scold - you simply do not get through to him; the only course is to remove him bodily from the scene until he has cooled down and then explain that he has hurt his victim; I even know one mother who went so far as to bite her child back, but I feel such measures are only a parent's prerogative! This kind of unpremeditated attack is just blind rage born of frustration, not calculated as a deterrent, and the attacker is often just as appalled as the victim afterwards. This is the time to explain to the culprit that if he is going to behave this way he cannot be allowed to go out and play with the others - he must stay where the teacher can keep an eye on him. Since most children prefer to play outside, this threat, easily enforceable, usually has the desired sobering effect and offers an incentive to future self control.

Tantrums are an inevitable problem with this age group,

though many children save these emotional outbursts for their parents rather than their teachers. On the rare occasions when these happened in school I left the child alone in an out-of-the-way corner until he got some control over himself, telling the others to leave him alone and he would soon feel better, treating the outburst rather as an embarrassing affliction than a crime. When the tempest had subsided, leaving the child wretched and somewhat ashamed of himself, I would take him on my lap and comfort him quietly until he felt better. It seemed pointless to be cross with him - after all the child suffered acutely as it was, and had no control over himself at the height of his rage. I felt he deserved sympathy; I just made sure that he never in fact achieved anything by his tantrums. In the course of time they subside.

To return to our free play session. At this early stage most of the play was experimental rather than any sustained make-believe. In the sandpit, for instance, individual children would be absorbed in investigating the properties of this strange new substance; they raked it, ran it through their fingers, packed it into buckets and sieves and tipped it out again, dug it and hammered it, tasted it and smelled it, poured water on it and jumped in it. Only later they used it to make roads and hills for their cars, or loaded it into their tip-up truck.

Similarly with water; floating boats was only an incidental activity as they threw everything they could find into the bath - sand, stones, bits of wood, toy cars, their shoes, anything that came to hand. They then observed that some things floated and some things did not, and that some things floated better than others. Then they solemnly watched the varying patterns as they churned up the water with an egg-whisk, poured it through a funnel or into a tin with holes in it. 'Pouring' was one of their chief delights. We had a collection of plastic mugs and a jug on a tray, and they would demonstrate with pride when they could pour out without spilling a drop on the tray. Sometimes we coloured the water just to add interest.

Blowing bubbles was another popular activity; a dozen plastic pipes and a large bowl of detergent kept everybody happy for an hour. When the weather was warm enough we filled the paddling pool with a hose - great delight this - and they all threw off their clothes with complete abandon and rushed in. On these days they had to be dragged home, protesting vigorously, at dinnertime.

Another thing of absorbing interest to them at this stage was their own increasing physical powers. With all the zeal and purpose of Olympic athletes they set themselves to achieve one goal after another: to run without falling on their noses, to work the pedal car and the tricycle, to climb the steps to the high slide and then dare to slither down it, to swing, to balance, to jump off the bench.

They were wholly absorbed in their own activities at that time, talking to themselves as they played, hardly ever playing with each other. Occasionally one of them would jam the policeman's hat on his head and decide to direct the traffic; the others would look up in surprise when he called to them to stop, but once they understood what was going on they joined in the game readily enough. Otherwise there was very little co-operative play until they were about four years old, though often a child would stand and stare with frank curiosity at something another child was doing, and then try to imitate him.

The Wendy House was very popular, but their activity there was usually confined to knocking on the door (that knocker never failed to fascinate them) and opening and shutting it: and then just sitting inside the house. They would pull the curtains across the window and then peep out, but obviously to them a house was a place to hide from the outside world.

The dolls were treated in a very cavalier manner - they were never really loved. Perhaps this is the fate of all communally-owned dolls. They liked taking the simple clothes on and off, and tucking them up in bed or pushing them round in the pram, though they preferred to ride in the pram themselves. Tea parties were frequent and elaborate, and always involved pouring out; this was another game where they did play in a group for short periods.

After our free play session, unless the weather was particularly inviting, we returned to the nursery for what was known as 'making'. Sometimes this was modelling with Plasticine or clay or dough - nice big satisfying lumps of it - sometimes paper folding and tearing or cutting with plastic scissors. Modelling equipment included solid wooden rolling pins, cutters of all shapes and sizes, a collection of things to imprint interesting patterns on the Plasticine (screws, shells, a fork, pencil stubs, little wheels). As with the sand and water, the children explored all the possibilities of this gorgeous squashy stuff, squeezing it, hammering it flat with their hands, rolling it into balls and sausages, and so on. There were one or two children who were afraid of getting their hands messy (too much emphasis on cleanliness at home?) and needed a lot of reassurance and persuasion before they would touch it. Once they realised that it could be cleaned off their hands afterwards, and that any mess could be cleaned off the tables and the floor, they just relaxed and enjoyed it.

The really uninhibited children loved finger-painting. We mixed powder paint with paste to a thick glutinous consistency and put blobs of different colours on to white oil-cloth. The children joyfully swirled this into exciting patterns, plunging both hands into the mess and rejoicing in the lovely blends of colour that they achieved. Afterwards a bowl of water quickly restored them and their surroundings to order.

Cutting with scissors, and even accurate tearing, are fairly skilled operations. Tearing is a very satisfying activity however, and to begin with I gave the children sheets of newspaper to tear into strips which they then rolled up for 'dolls' lavatory paper'. I instilled into them that they must only ever tear special paper given to them for the purpose, and I certainly never heard of them tearing up things they shouldn't - perhaps they no longer felt any need to. Paper folding, apart from very simple things like fans, was too complicated for them at this age, but they liked to fold ready-cut squares of thin paper in four, and then tear out bits to give a lacey effect when the paper was opened out. When they progressed to manipulating the little plastic paper scissors - sharp enough to cut paper but not fingers - they cut simple shapes like kites and squares and triangles out of coloured sticky-backed paper, and stuck them on to black sugar paper to make pictures. These were very rudimentary but gave enormous pleasure to the artists. We also made crowns and coloured them, Andy-Pandy hats out of paper bags, and soldier-hats out of newspaper with paper streamers. Small children wear such things with as much solemnity and confidence as their elders wear Paris creations; they certainly went home from school in some strange headgear.

One day I made them each a parachute from plastic bags; their delight was out of all proportion to the effort involved. After they had dropped them out of the nursery window a few times weighted with toy soldiers, Peter came puffing up to me in great excitement: 'Do you know why my soldier didn't bump?' he demanded breathlessly. 'It was the wind got inside his parachute - I saw it, and it sort of floated him.' Such is the satisfaction of the true scientist as one more bit of the puzzle clicks into place!

The last session of the morning was story-time, which in a way was the most important of all our activities in that it fed the children's minds with new ideas and consolidated their understanding of old ones. First of all we always got out the nursery rhyme book, an edition with beautiful pictures on every page which contained all the well-known rhymes and many delightful ones that were not so well known. Before long everybody knew nearly all of them, but far from detracting from their pleasure familiarity with the words added to the enjoyment of singing or saying them in unison. Each child chose his favourite and found the place in the book; they recognised the pictures, but even so young they were beginning too to pick out names and letters in the titles. I sat in the middle of the large old sofa with all the children round me so that they could all see the book, as I wanted them to connect the printed page with the pleasure of hearing stories and rhymes.

Then we had a story - or three or four, according to the time available. At this stage I avoided traditional folk stories, for reasons that I shall go into later. I told or read very simple stories about the everyday lives of children like themselves and the people they came into contact with, such as their families, the milkman and the postman. Animal stories were popular too, usually heavily anthropomorphised but this never worried the children.

At midday the mothers arrived to collect their young and to commiserate with me: 'You must be exhausted! What on earth do you do with all these children all morning?' On the first count they were quite wrong; I found being with children very peaceful and far less exhausting than doing housework; with them I was rarely tired and never bored. As for what I did with them all morning - well, it has taken a book to answer that one.

CHAPTER 3

Expansion

By the end of the first term I had quite a long waiting list, and at the same time a chance to expand spacewise. Our house was a very old one, with odd wings built on at various times through the ages, and beyond the workroom, though inaccessible except from the yard, was a big room that must originally have been a loft above the stables; at a later date some unknown artist had replaced the north wall with glass and used the place as a studio. By now it had degenerated into a storeroom for one of the shops on the High Street, but about this time the shop went bankrupt and was only too happy to hand back the tenancy of the loft.

This meant that we could now have a big classroom with its own entrance; the storeroom could do double duty as a cloakroom, and from there a small enclosed flight of stairs led directly up to the new room. Beside the cloakroom was an outside lavatory accessible from the yard. Once we had a door made between the workroom and the loft, this arrangement gave a suite of rooms - old nursery, workroom, new schoolroom - with a staircase and lavatory/washroom at either end; below were playroom, kitchen, and cloakroom-cum-storeroom, and we could still use the big drawing-room when we needed more space.

As soon as the children left for the summer holidays I set to work to convert the loft. It offered tremendous possibilities; it was rectangular in shape, some thirty feet long, with a high beamed roof. It was however in very bad condition. Cobwebs obscured the window, and layers of grime clung to the crumbling brick walls and the battered roof. We called in a friendly builder who soon dissipated my main worry in assuring me that the floor and staircase were sound and that the roof would not leak. One of the long walls was incurably damp; it was a thirteenth-century rubble wall of incredible thickness that ran right along one side of the house, and the only thing to do was to put a false wall of insulation board in front of it. This proved one of our greatest assets; it was soft enough to take drawing pins easily, so we had a display surface of some two hundred and seventy square feet for pictures. The crumbling lath and plaster ceiling we also clothed in insulation board and painted white; the beams, rough and grimy, looked better when stained to a decent dark oak. As well as the new door into the workroom the builder put in a wide window looking out over the yard and into the branches of one of the sycamore trees; it was low enough for the children to see straight out as they sat at the tables. The sycamore tree became a great feature of the place. In summer the sun streamed through its branches to make changing patterns in the gold-dust on the tables; in winter birds gathered on the bare twigs to come and feed on the windowsill without fear of the marauding cat below.

Over the well of the staircase we built a huge store-cupboard, big enough to take the reams of paper we needed, among other things; at the top of the stairs a little blue half-door to keep out the draughts and prevent us from stepping absent-mindedly backwards into the void. Right in the corner, curtained off in a little cubicle, the builder installed a mini-lavatory suited to the stature of its intended clientele. This would mean that I would not have to leave the other children when one of them needed assistance - there were always some thoughtless mothers who would dress their children in garments that they could not possibly manage for themselves. Also the child would not have to leave the group; often they were so afraid of missing something that they turned a deaf ear to the calls of nature until a perilously late hour. In practice this worked very well - the children would not usually even consent to draw the curtain decently, but continued to take part in the conversation from the corner. For the odd reticent member of the party there were two other lavatories and a clutch of pots available elsewhere that afforded more privacy.

One much-prized piece of equipment was an old foot-bath wheedled out of the groundsman at a local sportsground. It was a porcelain sink, but shallow and some two feet square. I had a low frame made to hold it at just the right height for the children. It was a simple matter to run cold water to it, and an electrician fixed me a second-hand water-heater above it. We fixed shelves, gaily covered in stick-on plastic, beside the sink to take the milk mugs and the water toys; deep shelves with an electric point above to take the record player, records, and percussion instruments; more shelves at the other end of the room to take toys, and later books.

Another great prize was in the form of an old shop counter, given to me by the chemist next door who was moving to another town. It was in rather wobbly condition, and had to be taken to pieces to get it up the stairs, being all of seven feet long, but its storage space was invaluable. It housed ten long drawers and five smaller ones as well as a really deep drawer for sewing things and a couple of shelves. My son reassembled it *in situ* and with a coat of paint, some new handles, and stick-on plastic on its top, it did valiant service for many years. Moreover its long top provided an excellent display surface for the innumerable models that we constructed in later years. It became known simply as 'the chest'.

The floor I covered in good tough lino, dark grey with a small geometrical pattern in bright colours, so that it would be cheerful without showing the dirt. Because there was no central heating in the house I invested in two childproof fan-heaters, which could equally well blow cold air in the summer if necessary. To begin with these were mounted on shelves high up out of the children's reach, but as they grew older we moved them down on to the floor as they seemed more effective that way. The smaller nursery and the workroom were also provided with enclosed fan-heaters - one of them could even be sat on without danger, and was a favourite perch of the more sybaritic members.

To perch on the bars of the window I made a felt parrot of many colours (Jezebel) and a small furry owl (Ooly); these two became our mascots and remained with us throughout the life of the school. Above the stairs, hung on a leather strap, I installed a Swiss cow bell to save my voice when I wanted to call in the stragglers down below. A generous length of fluorescent tube ensured adequate lighting on even the darkest of winter days.

It was all ready just in time for the start of the new term in September. At the last minute I mixed thirty pots of new paint and ranged them along the sill of the big north window to complete the décor. I also installed the newest resident, a goldfish named Albert, and scattered along the windowsill a collection of objects to interest the young and curious - a snowstorm in a glass dome, a magnet, a magnifying glass, an old clock and a watch with no back so that you could see its works, an egg-timer, a torch, a big shell in which you could hear the noise of the sea, a sealed test tube full of layers of different coloured sand from the Isle of Wight. In another corner was what was known as the 'fiddle board'. It was just an odd piece of wood on to which I had screwed all sorts of fittings used in joinery - a bolt, a turn-button, a hinge, an old-fashioned gate-latch, a hook and eye, a hasp and staple, padlock and key, and so on. It may sound an irrelevant piece of equipment, but small children are intrigued by the way such things work, and they spent ages doing them and undoing them until they really got the hang of them and the novelty wore off.

In this schoolroom the scene was set for five happy years. It was a place of colour and light, warmth and sunshine, peace and shelter; pattering feet, cries of excitement, contented humming, real laughter (as opposed to the artificial sort one hears so much more often). Remembering my own feet trailing so unwillingly to school, I loved to hear the children running eagerly down the passage to school in the morning, then the crash as they burst through the yard gate and came panting up the stairs to start a new day, full of plans of what they would do, and of anecdotes to share with the others.

By this second term, then, the premises, the equipment, the programme, were all working smoothly, and there were plenty of children, but the increasing problem was that of getting adequate help. Because some of the children only came one or two days a week there were fifteen or so on the books, and that should have meant fifteen possible helpers. I kept the fees very low in exchange for the promise of assistance from the mothers, but it inevitably meant that the same few did all the work, and on some days I could not persuade anyone at all to come. I could usually manage on my own well enough, but life became difficult if we had a new child who would not settle, and some of the children were very young.

Help eventually arrived in the shape of Margaret. At that time the local Nursery Nurses' Training School was sending its students out to nurseries all over the town for one day a week, to gain practical experience, and we were allotted to Margaret. She was still very young, but had what I regard as the essential qualities for working with children; she was endlessly patient, very sweet, and obviously liked being with children. Moreover she was very inventive, an inexhaustible source of ideas for games and for improvising equipment. When she finally qualified she came full time and set up with the youngest members in the old nursery, which henceforth became known as the Baby nursery.

The group was now beginning to assume a life of its own with a *modus vivendi* which the very young newcomers tended to disrupt, so we evolved a system whereby Margaret coped with the babies, the part-timers, and any really disruptive elements, painstakingly teaching them to fit into the community as I had done with the first-comers. She never had more than five or six in the Baby nursery, but that was quite enough, and she enjoyed being in charge of her own department; the children loved her.

Meanwhile I lived with the nine or ten older children in the schoolroom and watched them grow. The pattern of events was much the same, but their control and their understanding developed steadily. They no longer fumbled with the wooden screwdriver but could manipulate quite small metal nuts and bolts with dexterity. With the Matador they constructed complicated things like television cameras and tanks. They demanded harder and harder jigsaw puzzles – in fact there was one fiendishly difficult one which they could do a good deal faster than I could. With the tiny animals and figures that once their clumsy hands would have knocked over they now built villages and farms.

Once they had mastered the early fitting and grading toys they moved on to 'Matching cards'. These included picture dominoes (and later dot dominoes, where they have to count and match the dots) and picture lotto of various sorts, which encouraged fairly detailed observation of pictures and patterns and colours. We stocked a great many variations on this theme, to give everyone plenty of practice without tedious repetition, for this was an important part of the foundations of reading.

It was particularly interesting to watch their painting develop. Most of them chose to paint every day; by now they were much more adept with the brush and could produce something which satisfied them. A few of them were still at the stage of random blotches and lines for the sheer joy of creating colour, and others liked to cover the whole paper painstakingly with one colour, but most of them had progressed to recognisable pictures. These displayed two main subjects - people and houses. The people almost invariably consisted of huge heads with exaggerated saucer eyes, like flies, sometimes legs and arms protruding from the head, sometimes, but not always, a body (often with the navel conscientiously drawn in), and huge hands. I imagine that is what grown-up people look like to small children; when people bend down to them they must see only head and limbs, hardly the body at all. The eyes are obviously what they look at to determine whether the adult is angry, amused, sympathetic, or whatever - a principal means of communication before speech becomes easily understood. Hands too must assume great importance for a young child; first his mother's hands feeding him, washing and dressing him, giving him things; often at such close quarters that he does not see the rest of her; and later the teacher's hands on the table in front of him as she demonstrates a new toy, puts a piece in the puzzle, guides the pencil in his hand.

I could always tell from the child's paintings what sort of house he lived in. The children who lived in the centre of the town painted tall narrow houses with steep roofs, the ones from the new housing estates painted square houses with symmetrical windows and a little path going up to the front door. The ones from the older Victorian quarter of the town put steps going up to the front door and windows all over the place.

Gradually other things began to appear - trees beside the houses, not observed in any detail but always with a massive trunk and a blob of greenery somewhere way up at the top, again presumably the child's eye view of things. Animals were either friendly, with a Cheshire cat grin, or savage, with rows of huge jagged teeth. They too tended to be given a navel - obviously this was a feature of their own bodies which interested the children enormously.

It was some time later that the inevitable suns, complete with rays, began to appear like trademarks on all their paintings. I have never been able to account for this tiresome feature; I don't think children would notice the sun as much (it is not a thing one can stare at) but rather they would see sunshine as a diffused light without consciously noting where it comes from. I suppose they must pick up the habit from the stylised illustrations in so many children's books. Once the sun has arrived it seems to persist in their paintings right through the early years, until they are about six or seven, except in a few highly original children.

As well as picture painting the children now began to develop an interest in patterns for their own sake, from sheer delight in the juxtaposition of colours and the discovery of different ways of using the brush to make wavy lines, blobs, zigzags, and so on. At this stage I pointed out to them the patterns around them - on their clothes, on the floor coverings and curtains, on the end-pages of their books. Then we went on to the early writing patterns, done at first on huge sheets of paper with brushes, felt pens, or chalk; these are patterns repeating the basic letter shapes in horizontal lines from left to right across the page. As well as being fun to do and attractive to look at when finished, these lay the foundations of fluent writing. For one thing the child forms the habit of moving across the page evenly and in the right direction (by no means instinctive) and in a continuous controlled flow. For another, he is learning the basic movements needed to form the individual letters. (*Figure 1*) This activity

we carried on regularly for years until the children were writing a good cursive hand, but as they went on the paper and the tool became smaller and the patterns more precise.

Later on we used to do 'picture writing', rhythmical patterns as we chanted rhymes together. The idea here was to learn to make repeated identical shapes quickly and easily without stopping to draw each one laboriously.

There was a little bird with an egg-shaped body

His little round head went nod- nod- noddy,

He'd a little yellow beak for pecking up his food

And two little legs for running round the wood.

You can draw one row of birds, adding a new feature each line.

Or again:

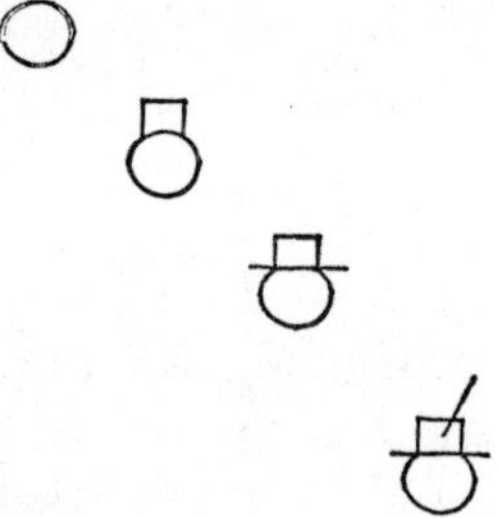

One day I met a little man whose
  face was very fat,
To crown it all, upon his head he
  wore a little hat;
Around the hat there was a brim,
  and that was very thin,
And through the hat, to hold it on,
  he'd stuck a silver pin.

And so on ad infinitum; I amused myself inventing endless reams of such doggerel as the need arose.

Sometimes this developed into what we called 'story

patterns'. I would begin a story by setting a scene which the children would illustrate on a large sheet of paper as I went along (*Figure 3*), something like this:

Once upon a time there was a castle with walls so long that you could hardly see the ends of them (pause while the bricks are drawn in).

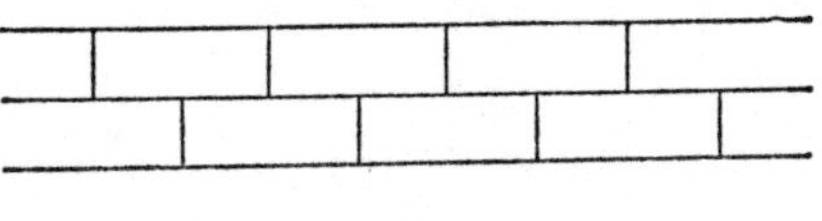

On top of the wall were the battlements, like square holes for the soldiers to peep through,

and above the battlements you could just see the heads of the soldiers,

with their tall
helmets,
and their spears.

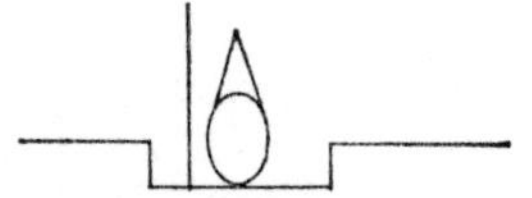

At the bottom of the walls
was a deep moat,

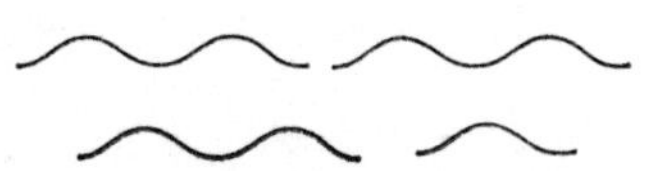

and curled up in front of the moat was the longest monster you ever saw,

with horns,

and evil little eyes,

and a spikey tail

and hundreds of feet. 

- and so on

Once they had mastered the knack of drawing geometrical shapes they went on to build these up into pictures, as with the bird in the picture writing. Sometimes after several abortive attempts someone would ask despairingly: 'How do you draw a horse (dog, lion, or whatever)?' Then we would all try to think of a horse, and I would prompt them with questions - 'What sort of a head does he have? A round head, a long head, a fat head, a narrow head?' After discussion they would decide that it had a long head. 'And what about its body? Round, or long and thin? A rectangle or a square? What sort of ears? Long, short, pointed, rounded?' - and so on until we had built up a composite picture of basic shapes. Though the drawings were still rudimentary they were beginning to get the shape and proportions right, and gradually they learned to round them out and add the details.

We also built up pictures on felt-boards with pre-cut felt shapes - I cut my own, much larger than those supplied commercially, in shapes calculated to inspire pictures, such as triangles of various sorts, half-circles, cloud shapes, lozenges, and so on, in a wide variety of colours. Sometimes we used small felt shapes repetitively to build up patterns.

We did a great deal of drawing, not as early 'art' training but as a valuable means of communication and self-expression before the children could read and write. When this happened their creativeness was largely transferred to their free writing and most of them lost interest in painting and drawing, though they always enjoyed illustrating a story or a poem (I wonder whether this was when they felt their word power still inadequate to the particular need).

We never traced or copied drawings, apart from the odd occasions when we particularly wanted accuracy, and filling in fiddling line drawings always seems to me a waste of time. Sometimes they drew round cardboard geometrical shapes and carefully filled in the outline in solid colour with a big wax crayon, then cut out the shapes and carried them proudly home. This was a particularly popular activity when they were struggling to gain control of their hands, and it certainly gave them practice in accuracy.

With paper cutting and folding we became much more ambitious; we also used paste and shapes cut out of colour magazines, or out of material, to make collage pictures. These were usually group efforts (to which even the youngest could contribute), producing a much more impressive result from the child's point of view. For instance, if the subject was a bowl of flowers, the youngest ones would tear up pink and blue paper and stick it on to the bowl shape (already outlined) in a random mosaic pattern. The more deft would tear or cut out flower shapes from two or three other colours and paste these on to the background, finally drawing in the stalks and leaves with crayon or charcoal.

One such effort the children loved so much that it stayed on the walls for years, they could not bear to part with it. I painted a tree with white paint on black paper; the children divided into two groups, one to cut leaves from gold foil, the other to cut paper birds which they coloured brightly and perched among the branches. It was certainly very effective.

We did a great deal of this sort of work, so that by the age of four all the children who had been with us for any length of time were able to use scissors, and cope with paint and paste without getting in a mess.

Woodwork was not so successful. Most of them could bang in nails with a fair degree of accuracy, and remove unwanted ones with pincers, but sawing seemed to be beyond them until the age of six or thereabouts. Because of this they were very limited in what they could make, having to use the pieces of wood just as they were since they could not shape them. They made the inevitable ships by nailing several layers of wood together, but then they became frustrated because they could not carry out the more grandiose schemes they had in mind. I helped them to a certain extent, but the activity lost its point if I did all the work.

Modelling became increasingly popular, and the children progressed from marbles and sausages to creating imaginary animals, baskets of fruit and vegetables, loaves and cakes, and little men. They developed to good effect their earlier technique of printing patterns with anything that came to hand, and so produced dragons with regular rows of scales, cups and plates with shell patterns round the edges, oranges covered in pinpricks, and other such carefully observed details. We mostly used Plasticine, in balls the size of a child's fist and, like the paint, in as many clear bright colours as we could find. At this stage we kept the colours separate because nothing looks less appetising than the grey mud-colour of mixed-up Plasticine. We used clay too, in bigger lumps, and made coil pots and thumb pots as well as fanciful animals. We also used dough - this was very popular. Besides cutting and rolling to their heart's content they delighted in making loaves and cakes and pies for a play-bakery. This dough contained a lot of salt as a preservative and was not for eating; it was painted, baked for a long time in a slow oven, and then varnished. Occasionally we made real pastry, and then we turned out trays of jam tarts which we baked in the kitchen and consumed as soon as they were cool enough.

We experimented with papier mâché too, but this was not very successful at this age. It was rather a lengthy process and the children lost interest halfway through the project, but I wanted them to have some experience of it so that they could use it later if they wanted to.

In the workroom we had a large box known as the 'junk-box'. It contained egg-cartons, cotton reels, corks, tops of toothpaste tubes, silver paper, cardboard, corrugated paper, cotton wool, scraps of crêpe paper, date boxes, walnut shells, the insides of toilet rolls, empty cartridge cases, empty vaccine bottles begged from the doctor, pipe-cleaners, matchboxes, old plastic bottles, cocktail sticks, and anything else that anyone thought might come in useful. We also stocked unlimited supplies of Sellotape, paper fasteners, and tubes of glue. This collection, always available to anyone who happened to be feeling creative, inspired a variety of models ranging from the incomprehensible to the truly ingenious, scientific, artistic, or purely functional, but all a source of great pride and satisfaction to their inventors. In children of this generation who take bought toys so much for granted it bred a spirit of invention and improvisation, and in later years they were never at a loss for ideas or skills when it came to model making or devising equipment for their games.

Outside, their physical prowess increased month by month. The child who at first gazed in wonder at the climbing apparatus but preferred to remain on terra firma himself, was eventually to be seen swinging like Tarzan on ropes and monkey swing, or weaving in and out of obstacles (human and vehicular) as he chased after his companions with surprising speed and dexterity. I encouraged them to jump over ropes and off boxes, to throw and catch beanbags (much easier than balls), to push and pull each other in carts, to kick big balls around. On average the boys developed much more slowly at this stage than the girls.

Watching them all I realised that it is a considerable feat of balance and co-ordination to hop on one foot, or to skip along (without a rope). Though most of the girls could skip, as a dancing step, by the age of three or four, some children just could not get the knack of this before they were five or even six. It was changing feet that floored them; they would step and hop, then start off again on the same foot. It is possible that the girls' faster progress in this direction was something to do with their greater interest in dancing. Most of them loved it and went to some sort of dancing class outside school one afternoon a week. One or two boys went too and they seemed to enjoy it as much as anyone. I think the reason why more boys don't go to dancing class is simply one of social pressure - it 'isn't done', or their mothers think it effeminate - which is a pity, because in school the boys get just as much fun out of it as the girls.

From time to time I tried to get the children interested in puppets, but without much success as far as their own activity was concerned. On the other hand they loved it when Margaret or I put on a show for them. These shows were very simple, of the Punch and Judy variety, and made up as we went along. With the aid of an old blanket as backdrop the Wendy House could be converted easily into a theatre, and we soon found ourselves giving a performance every morning. The children would pull some benches and boxes into position in front of the Wendy House and just sit there shouting joyfully for 'Mr Punch' until one of us dived behind the curtain and tried to think up something new.

There was great audience participation in the form of question and answer, howling down the villain, anxious warnings to the victim, and advice freely given on all occasions. They seemed to forget, or even to be unaware, of us behind the curtain, and to become completely involved with the characters. Perhaps that is why they never wanted to manipulate the puppets themselves. Of course they wanted to look behind the curtain afterwards, but they seemed rather disappointed and puzzled to find nothing there except the lifeless puppets. Some children would put the puppets on their hands and play with them for a little while, or even install themselves behind the curtains and half-heartedly jerk the characters to life, but it was not until much later that they took any real interest in giving their own performances.

Sometimes I put a puppet on my hand and told a story about it, making the puppet act the part; on these occasions the children listened attentively, with round eyes riveted on the puppet, but not many of them wanted to touch it; they stood in awe of it in some way, as if they could not quite understand what it was.

Books were becoming increasingly significant in all our activities, as entertainment, as inspiration for games and pictures, and simply for information. I continued to tell or read a wide variety of stories every day, and also we spent a lot of time just looking at picture books and talking about them. They opened up whole new worlds to the children, whose experience at that age was necessarily very limited. Often they would be able to fill in the gaps for each other. I remember two boys studying together a book about a farm and discussing one particular picture.

'What's that funny house?'

'It isn't a house, it's a haystack.'

'What's that for then?'

'Well they put the hay there and they cover it up with a black mackintosh so that it doesn't get rained on.' - And as an afterthought: ' - and mice live in it.'

Obviously experience talking here. Then another child chipped in: 'The hay is for horses to eat.'

By this time everybody had gathered round to look.

'I've seen hay growing,' proffered someone nonchalantly; 'and it's just grass really.' At this point I added as much information as I deemed necessary to clarify the matter, and made a mental note to point out hayfields and haystacks next time we were in the country.

One valuable function of the picture books was simply to extend vocabulary. When my own two sons were very small they loved the 'Rupert' books, and we spent hours poring over these while they pointed to various objects and I supplied the noun - or alternatively I pointed and they proudly 'told'. This was long before I read the stories to them - rather we deduced the story together from the pictures. I think they both learned to talk from 'Rupert'.

More and more the children wanted to know about the writing under the pictures. 'What does it say?' was a constant cry. I would pick out the most significant word, 'cat' if the picture was about a cat, and sound it out for them. In this way they came to connect the shape of the letter with the sound it made, and were soon picking out sounds and letters for themselves. I never taught them the alphabetical names for the letters - this seems to me to add quite unnecessary confusion.

When they began to show an interest in words, I stapled up sheets of paper into books for them to make their own picture books. On each page they would draw, or cut out and paste in, a picture of a single object - a fish, a house, a cat - and I would print the name underneath. I did not encourage them to try and write themselves at first, though some of them did try of their own accord. They were very proud of these books and would keep going back over them and 'reading' the words under the pictures. There was always a box of scrap-pictures on the shelf - cut from magazines or bought by the sheet - and the craze for making picture books with them caught on in a big way.

All the time they were getting a clearer understanding of number and I introduced as much practice as possible into our activities. Counting songs and games helped, but free play was more valuable. They set the table for four dolls, counting out four plates, four cups, four knives, four serviettes, and so on. They played shops and bought four apples in exchange for four pennies. They drew animals with four legs, and constructed cars with four wheels, and after all that they knew very well what four meant. At this stage, and not before, I introduced the written symbol for four, for them to recognise, not for them to write yet. When they knew the numbers up to six they enjoyed doing number-matching puzzles. These took a variety of forms, but the object was always to match a collection of objects to a corresponding number. A variation was for a child to collect the objects himself, count them, and add a ticket which bore the corresponding number; sometimes he built a farm or zoo with enclosures, put animals in them and labelled the enclosures with the number of animals; sometimes it was a group of trees (cut from green card with Plasticine bases) in a park, or cakes on a plate (counters on a tin lid), or conkers in boxes, or children on benches (pipe-cleaner figures on a building brick).

It was fascinating to watch a child playing with Lego, a very popular toy from about three and a half upwards. If he was building a house, he would build one wall with five bricks, then would count out five bricks from the box before he began to build the other side of the house - obviously aware of the numerical length of his house though one would say that he could not have counted them.

We had at that time a charming counting-frame - quite the nicest I have ever come across. It had ten horizontal wires, each with ten beautifully shaped little wooden birds on it. Each row had five birds of one colour and five of another, with the details picked out in silver. We had a lot of fun with those birds, counting them as they shuffled along the wire or back to the nest. With them the children first explored the concepts of addition and subtraction.

But we did not spend all our time in the schoolroom. When the sun shone we went to the parks nearby and fed the ducks, collected conkers, looked for the first buds. In winter we fed the birds, put water out to freeze and watched it bulge over the top of the bottle, marvelled over the frost patterns on the window, gloated over snowstorms. In spring we looked for primroses and pussy-willows, watched the chestnut buds open in the warmth of the room. In the summer we went for picnics in the woods or on the farm (for we had found that most valuable ally, a friendly farmer), and picked flowers to decorate the schoolroom. In the autumn we collected berries and planted bulbs - these as they grew were a never-failing source of wonder. We also grew mustard and cress in vast quantities in the airing cupboard, and carrot tops on the windowsill,[1] and made dish-gardens with moss and pebbles, twigs and flowers.

The first time I ventured out to the park with my charges I found it an unnerving experience. I had taken the precaution of asking one of the mothers to come with me. We

[1] Cut half an inch from the top of a carrot and place in a shallow dish containing water about quarter of an inch deep. You can also add a layer of pebbles to make it look nicer. Be sure to keep the water topped up.

piled as many of the children as possible into two large and ancient prams for the short journey to the park, thinking to conserve their energies for later. This proved a mistake; we should have worn them out on the way there, for no sooner had we released them than they scattered in all directions, whooping joyfully as they disappeared into the distance - it was a large park. I don't think we ever should have rounded them up again if one of them had not discovered some swings; one by one the others noticed her and came to join the fun, so eventually we had them all within reach once more. After that we carried a whistle and taught them to respond to it like dogs.

One of our liveliest outings in these early days was when the circus came to town. We thought it would be nice to take the children to visit the menagerie one morning when it would not be too crowded. As usual one or two public-spirited parents volunteered help and transport, but when the morning arrived the rain poured down in torrents. The children were so much looking forward to the trip that we were loath to disappoint them; we rang up the circus and were told that the menagerie was still open despite the weather, so we decided to go anyway as it would be mostly under cover.

When we arrived the circus ground was under water. Kindly circus men laid planks across the mud for us, and finally carried all the children across the flood to the animal tent, which all added to the excitement. The visit was a great success; we spent an hour or so gazing at the animals, who gazed back at us in some astonishment. The trouble really began when it was time to go home. The men helped us once more over the worst of the flood and left us with cheerful farewells to pick our way round the edge of the field to the road. Most of the children were wearing wellingtons and were in the seventh heaven of delight sloshing through deep puddles and bogs, but others were more nervous and picked their way precariously, getting horribly wet and messy in the process. The climax came when one small girl fell flat on her nose in the mud: when we had prised her out of the mire, howling dismally, she was coated from head to foot in black slime. Though very sympathetic we could not help laughing - but she was not amused.

Then we found ourselves cut off from the road by a paling fence. Our hearts sank at the prospect of going all the way back across the bog - all the children were getting pretty tired and uncomfortable by this time - so one enterprising father tried to force a gap in the fence. Just as he was on the point of succeeding it gave way and he was precipitated head-first into the next field, one more victim of the mud. By that time we had just given up caring. We hoisted the miserable children over the fence as best we could to the muddy figure on the other side, then we squeezed through ourselves and landed in the mud too; the whole enterprise had taken on the aspect of slapstick comedy. We must have presented a hilarious picture to the reception party back at school, where drier and cleaner parents than us waited to carry their off-spring home to dinner. I am bound to say that they were pretty good about the state of their children's clothes.

As the year rolled round we marked the seasons in our own way - parties at Christmas, fireworks on Bonfire Night, Easter eggs at the end of the spring term. The first year I had the bright idea of hiding the eggs in a straw nest on which nestled a large and rather grotesque paper hen of my own making. This was greatly appreciated; the hen was the object of much interest and admiration, and the children went off home for the holidays relating the surprising phenomenon to their parents in excited voices. I forgot all about it until the last day of the following spring term, when I overheard a whispered confabulation about whether anyone had seen the hen sitting on her nest yet - of course she would be there, just as she had been last year. I was mortified. Of course I had Easter eggs for them, but no hen. It was unthinkable to disappoint them, so I got Margaret to draw them all off to watch Punch and Judy while I rapidly knocked up a replica of last year's hen and nest. So when the childern clustered round expectantly at the end of the morning there indeed was the hen in all her glory, and if she was rather more roughly executed than the original nobody seemed to notice.

One event that is scored deep into my memory is the Nativity Play. I am not a great lover of nativity plays, particularly from the organising end; but I know that the Christmas story weaves its magic anew over every generation, and if acting it out helps them to understand it better, who am I to cast a jaundiced eye over their efforts? Unfortunately it has become a ritual, a performance where the children feel that they are on show, and the tension and neurotic rehearsals beforehand are liable to ruin everyone's enjoyment. However, parents do seem to like watching their offspring looking cherubic (and usually quite out of character), so we decided that we would have a Nativity play, but that it would be largely unrehearsed. The ages of the actors ranged between two and four, so on the whole rehearsals would have been ineffective anyway.

For a few weeks before the event we taught them half a dozen carols, and kept on telling them the Nativity story in different ways. We 'played' the story, dressed up for the parts, and talked about it, and drew pictures of it, until by the end of term everybody knew it backwards. Then we told them that tomorrow their Mummies and Daddies would come and they could play the story again for them to see. Also we would sing some carols and maybe the audience would join in.

We disguised the Wendy House as a stable, mocked up a fire for the shepherds out of twigs and red paper, and sat back. Nothing could go wrong - the children had done all this lots of times before and would be quite natural. Alas! We had reckoned without the effect of the audience. The children immediately became self-conscious. The shepherds either remained staring gloomily into the fire or mumbled their comments inaudibly into their dressing-gowns. There was one tense moment when they had a sharp difference of opinion about the ownership of one of the lambs, so we hastened on the Angel Gabriel to make her historic announcement. Normally she made this in suitably dramatic ringing tones, but on this occasion she remained silently dominating the shepherds, arms crossed on her chest in the proper angelic manner. After an uncomfortable pause I murmured encouragingly from behind the scenes: 'Well go on, tell them what has happened.' At this she burst loudly into tears and bawled 'I don't want to!' There were no curtains to draw discreetly at this moment, so I led the sobbing Gabriel behind the stable, mopped her up and tried to calm her down. Soon there were rebellious mutterings from inside the curtained stable where Joseph and Mary were waiting to be revealed, and one of the shepherds wanted to go to the lavatory. I explained the urgency of the situation to the Angel, who with a desperate sniff pulled herself together and sallied forth to collect up the shepherds, her halo awry and her nose running - but I took my hat off to her; never did an actress rise to the occasion better in an emergency. We took the Angel's message as read and the play proceeded, but by this time the audience was in a state of ill-concealed hilarity. Joseph played the gangling ineffectual father to perfection; Mary was prim, and dealt sharply with the shepherds, who were reluctant to hand over the lamb. Then we sang 'We three kings', and after much prodding the kings wandered out from their retreat behind a curtain - they had lost interest in the proceedings long ago and were engrossed in some game of their own. They were quite bemused to find themselves in the public eye and wandered three times round the stable until Mary, with great presence of mind, snatched the first king's gold offering; he stopped in surprise and the other two promptly fell over him. While taking charge of the other gifts in a business-like manner she absent-mindedly dropped the baby on the floor, where Joseph stood gazing at it in a worried manner, but obviously thought it best not to interfere. The closing carol gave the parents time to pull themselves together and make the proper noises of appreciation and admiration; at this the children brightened up enormously and were all for doing the whole thing again, but here I put my foot down - I had had as much as I could take for one morning.

CHAPTER 4

The Pickley Wizard

My own elder daughter Deborah had been in the school since it started when she was two and a half years old, and soon after her fourth birthday I began to feel that she had worked her way through all the nursery activities and was now ready for something more to bite on. She was still very happy in the mornings with the other children, but she had grown tired of the toys and spent all her time poring over the books and trying to pick out the letters and sounds. Obviously the time had come to teach her to read, but since I could not take time in the mornings to devote to her alone, we saved this activity for the afternoons. My younger daughter, Rebecca, was not yet two and still had a long rest in her cot in the afternoons; so during this time every day Deborah and I settled down with the reading book. It was a session which we both greatly enjoyed and she made rapid progress. I was anxious to complete the task before she went to school, where they would almost certainly use different methods of teaching; this would confuse her dreadfully if she was still only halfway through the process. In fact it took us three months from start to finish - at four and a half she could read anything fluently, including *The Times*, though whether she understood the meaning of what she read depended on whether the subject matter fell within the compass of her own experience.

I did not attempt to teach her to write, because at that age her hand control was hardly adequate, and I knew I had not time to complete the process before she went to school; better to leave it to them. She already had a good understanding of number, but I had not begun any formal number work with her.

When she was four and a half I felt the time had come for her to go to school; ours was after all only a nursery school, and all the other children would have to go on to proper school at five (several of them had already done so), and several of the younger ones would be returning home to America and Canada during the summer.

So after Easter off she went to school, full of excitement and yearning to get on with some real 'work'. Alas! Like her mother before her, she was doomed to disappointment. Most schools, unfortunately, just aren't like that. Because she could read she was put into a class of six-year-olds; this was a major mistake to begin with. She did not make many friends, and I do not suppose they took very kindly to this small thing being detailed off to hear their stumbling efforts at reading to save the teacher's time. One bright spot on the horizon was that in the classroom were a lot of books she had not read, but to her chagrin she was rationed to one or two a week in case she got through them too fast.

Writing was on the timetable, but this seemed to consist of being left to trace letters on her own - very boring and tiring, and it does not really teach you very much. Arithmetic was rather a bore too; the class had got on to tens and units, and since nobody thought to explain this to her she was completely mystified as to what they were all doing.

School was undoubtedly a flop, and there did not seem much prospect of it improving in the foreseeable future. Moreover if it was a flop for Deborah, the same fate would seem to be in store for all the other lively youngsters who were due to move on to school in the coming months. They too were full of curiosity and eagerness to learn, used to being interestingly occupied every minute of their time in school; none of them would take kindly to sitting still at desks all morning, waiting endlessly for the teacher to attend to them or for the slowest child to finish. It made me bitter to think of their bright eyes growing dull with boredom, of their curiosity and eagerness blunted by frustration. Of course they would become resigned to it in the end like the rest of us; some of them would turn to naughtiness as a relief from their boredom, and be branded as difficult unco-operative children - how often I have seen this happen, when it was the teacher who should have been castigated for failing to do her job properly.

There were of course other schools in the town, but none that sounded as though it could cope with the problem - I had inside information on most of them, either because I had taught there, or knew members of the staff well enough to discuss the matter frankly with them, or had friends whose children were there.

In a way too I had created this particular problem myself. These children were further developed than most children of their age, but since they had arrived at this point by entirely natural means without any pushing on my part (all I did was to provide the conditions for them to develop freely) I am convinced that this was an entirely right and good thing, to be fostered at all costs.

At all costs - there's the rub! I am a realist, and I knew that if I was really concerned that these children should have the sort of education that I had dreamed up for them, I should have to provide it myself. I was rather appalled by the idea at first. What if it did not come off? Was it not an awful risk to take, particularly with my own children? I discussed it with one or two teaching friends; their reaction boiled down to: 'What fun, to have your own school - every teacher's dream; but not for your own children. You cannot possibly be teacher and mother to them.' I thought about the joy I had experienced in teaching my own children to read, and their ready response, and I wondered why my friends were so adamant on this point. Why are most teachers so convinced that they must suppress any maternal instincts when dealing with the children they teach? This renders them less than human - a different sort of being from the adults the child knows in normal life; little wonder if he is then unable to treat them as quite human. My own experience convinces me that it is this very sympathy and warmth - love if you like an old-fashioned word - which evokes in return the trust and affection of the child, the only proper relationship between two people who have to work together in such close harmony. It is only after this relationship is firmly established that I feel I can begin to teach a child effectively. The only other possible bases are fear, which may make for some effective learning but is very limited and wholly undesirable; and interest, which is not enough for young children, to whom confidence in the teacher is of prime importance.

Apart from the problem of my own two children, the temptation to run my own school was enormous. To be able to try out my theories in practice, just to see what happens when children are set free from the restrictions of normal school life to develop at their own pace, to explore in whatever direction their curiosity takes them; free from fear, as far as it is humanly possible to make it, in an atmosphere which is an extension of home. Being a realist I also saw that it would take all my time and energies for the next five years, and that there would be endless snags and frustrations; but I knew in a vague sort of way that it was what I had always wanted to do anyway, and in the end I could not resist the challenge.

One important aspect of an ideal education is continuity, and I was already beginning to see the effects of this at nursery school level. It was the children who came at three years old and stayed on that were showing the surprising rate of development, and the coming and going of the others, though inevitable, tended to disturb the harmony of the group. Up to this time a large proportion of our children were drawn from the families of overseas students who were engaged on post-graduate studies at the University. This gave us an interesting mixture of nationalities and backgrounds - American, Canadian, Australian, New Zealanders, German, Dutch, and Swiss - but it also meant that they were here only for short periods and we lost them just as we were getting to know them; the turnover was too great for stability.

I wanted to collect a group of children ranging from Deborah's age to Rebecca's who would stay together for several years - only then would it be possible to evaluate the effects of their education. I was often asked whether I handpicked the children. The answer to this is no, but I must plead guilty to selecting the parents very carefully. It was very important that the parents should be wholly identified with what I was trying to do with their children. In the odd cases where the parents did not understand or trust my methods, which were after all a bit unorthodox, their attitude affected the child and he was never able to integrate fully with the group. This was nobody's fault, but without the parents' co-operation half the value of my particular sort of teaching was lost, and the group was more comfortable without them. Apart from this the group presented the usual range of ability and problems - the one thing they had in common was that their parents were passionately interested in them and deeply concerned with their education.

One thing that worried me at the beginning was whether the boys would find the conditions a bit too cramping in our rather confined premises. There were three of them in the new group, all of whom had been in the nursery school since the age of two or three, but they were coming up to the rumbustious age when a ten-acre field would have been more appropriate than our backyard. In the end the lack of alternatives decided the question and they stayed until they finally went to prep school at the age of eight. I was always so grateful that they did; they added an element of fun and high spirits without which our life together would have been much the poorer.

Opening a proper school is a rather more complicated business than starting a nursery school. For one thing we passed from the jurisdiction of the Health Department to that of the Department of Education and Science, and would have to satisfy Her Majesty's Inspector of Schools of our competence. It meant too, a considerable outlay on books and teaching equipment - in fact the place had to be put on to a viable financial footing (I still had hardly begun to pay back my father's £200). Since I was a teacher by trade there was no problem about my qualifications for the job, but I would have to satisfy the authorities that the premises and equipment were adequate for the number of children. Not that there was any restriction on the number of children I could take - considering the outrageous overcrowding in many state schools the government would have found it difficult to justify any such regulation - but in any case I had no intention of taking more than I could teach properly.

The next hurdle was the visit of the HMI, but he turned out to be a dear and the children took to him in a big way, which was merciful; if they had taken a dislike to him anything might have happened. They did not seem to realise the deference due to an HMI; I remember on a subsequent visit they were making witch-hats for their Hallowe'en party; they greeted him with joy and, clamping a witch-hat on his head, whirled him into a wild Hallowe'en dance. Fortunately he took their high spirits in good part.

The only thing we now needed to complete the formalities was a name. This deficiency had been tackled at various parents' meetings, but apart from a few ribald and untenable suggestions nobody had ever come up with anything feasible - apart from the 'Pickley Wizard', which had stuck as a sort of joke. It had originated in the early days of the nursery when Jimmy had asked me to draw him a pickley wizard. I did my best, but it was obviously not what was wanted, and after a few rather desperate attempts which proved equally wide of the mark Jimmy got really mad and started asking less stupid people to draw what he wanted. Soon everyone was drawing wizards - with and without hats, in and out of pickle jars, eating pickles, growing out of a pickled onion like Venus rising from the foam - until the thing had assumed a presence of its own and positively haunted the place. By the time someone discovered that what Jimmy was really on about was a prickly lizard, the thing had come to live with us for good. So when the question of a name for the school came up once again, someone said, 'What about "The Pickley Wizard"?' and *faute de mieux* that's what it was. It was a name that intrigued Americans and they came along just to see what sort of a place it could be with a name like that; they usually liked what they saw and stayed. It was another matter when it came to registering the school with the Department of Education and Science, but I wanted to get the application form off and I could not think of anything better - anyway I had become rather attached to the name by that time. So 'The Pickley Wizard' was duly registered as an independent school (probably the smallest in England) and ever afterwards I received Government circulars pompously addressed to 'The Principal, The Pickley Wizard'.

We now felt we were launched and we celebrated with a parents' party which marked the beginning of a long and close association between us. The Pickley Wizard was launched as, and remained throughout, a parents' co-operative for the education of their own children.

For the first year after Deborah's return to the fold we were still phasing out the remnants of the nursery school. Margaret continued to look after the younger children in the Baby nursery, which by now included Rebecca and three other children of the same age who would later join me in the schoolroom as members of the permanent establishment. These were Isobel, Nicky, and Sebastian (known as Sebbie in those days because he was much too small for such a long name). Like Rebecca they were between two and three years old; Sebbie had already been with us for six months.

In the schoolroom the permanent group was already forming. Besides Deborah, who was just five, were three children a few months younger, Jose, Catherine, and Graham; they had joined us at the age of three. During that year Michela arrived, and then two sisters Candy and Clare; Candy was the same age as Deborah, the other two a few months younger. The group was eventually completed by Catherine's younger sister Elwyn, Edward, and Antonia - these three were a bit younger than Rebecca, so in the end there were fourteen children with an age range of just three years between oldest and youngest. Various other children came and went, but these fourteen formed the closely-knit continuous group that reflected the cumulative effect of five or six years' teaching.

For that first year I gave most of my attention to teaching the four year olds to read. With Graham, Jose and Catherine, who had been in the nursery for some time and had been through all the pre-reading stages, this came easily and quickly. Michela, whose mother taught her at home, soon caught up with them; but Candy and Clare found it much more difficult and we simply had to start and lay the foundations that they had missed and then proceed much more slowly.

Once a child had passed through all the fitting and grading toys, picture-matching and so on, he was usually anxious to tackle reading for himself. At this point I began to teach the sounds of the letters. We had an alphabet frieze round the walls, and to avoid the standard confusion of the child's supposing that somehow h means the same as the word hen, we would always think up as many examples as possible of words that begin with h, to drive home the point that we were only talking about the initial sound. Some of the children had already been taught the alphabetical names of the letters, and this caused them great confusion. As long as they called the letter aitch instead of huh it bore no relation to the word hen. Once the letter sounds had been learnt we went on to word-building. We had a set of plastic lower-case letters for this - capital letters were another home-aid that we could have done without. When parents decide to teach their children their letters it is nearly always the capitals that they teach them, though these are used very little in printed books and should be learned after the much more useful lower-case letters. We played all sorts of games with these letters; I would put down *at* on the table, and someone had to add another letter to make a word. Perhaps she would produce *cat*, then the next child had to replace one letter and make a different word. Sometimes it was my turn to change the letters and they had to read the word I had made. I began with only a few letters and gradually added the rest. This word-building and phonetic practice went on for a year or two as a separate exercise from reading until the children were absolutely sure of phonetic spelling; it may not solve the problem of reading when the language happens to be English, but it provides at least the key to the vast majority of words.

As soon as the child could recognise all the letter sounds he began on his first reading book. I chose the Ladybird Key Word series, though there were many other good ones to choose from. I liked this system because the pictures were good and clear and attractive; moreover they talk about things that children are interested in, the everyday doings of children like themselves, extended to include all the things they would like to do if they had the chance. A visitor once criticised them on the grounds that they were so ordinary and uninspiring - thereby missing the whole point of them. Later on children yearn for the magical, the excitement of adventure, but at five they are more interested in the world they know but have not yet fully explored. In these Key Word books the author has worked out, in order of frequency, the most used words in the English language, and he introduces them systematically into the books a few at a time. These words we learned by the 'look-and-say' method - that is, to recognise them at sight without stopping to work them out phonetically. To help the learning process we played games with cards bearing the individual words from the book (known as 'flash-cards' in the trade), built up sentences with them, matched them to pictures and so on. Even though many words are not phonetically logical at least a knowledge of phonetics helps a faulty memory.

There were enough readers for each child to have his own copy, and each one worked through them at his own pace. I took each child individually for a daily reading lesson, and when I found that this was taking more time than I could spare from the rest of the class, I called upon the mothers to come and help. They formed a rota, and someone came each morning for the sole purpose of hearing each child read until he himself decided that he had done enough. If he had decided that he did not want to read at all that day he would not have been pressed, but I do not remember it ever happening. They were all tremendously enthusiastic about reading and would not have missed their private session for anything.

An unforeseen snag arose when these four year olds reached book 6 of the readers. The text had been increasing in length with each successive book, and by now the printing was down to normal size. As each of the children arrived at this book she complained that she could not see it properly, that the lines all jumbled together. The intended reading age of book 6 is six and a half to seven years, by which time the child's eyes would be considerably more developed, but at four they all found the print trying. I have noticed too that when young children are choosing books for themselves they reject the ones with 'normal' print and go for the ones with large clear letters and wide spacing.

So we stopped the Key Word series at book 6, returning to the others later, and went on to other elementary readers, as wide a variety as possible to widen the vocabulary, and soon after this the children were, for their own practical purposes, reading fluently.

There is always a gulf between the ability to read and the confidence to tackle new books by oneself. To bridge this the children went on having individual reading lessons, but chose their own books; soon they wanted to know the next bit of the story and read it on their own. Once they realised that they could do this they were away, and began reading longer and longer stories. By the age of five several of them were voracious readers and were enjoying full length Puffins and Ladybirds.

As they finished each reader they were given a small prize to mark the occasion. I am a firm believer in bribery - or incentives, to use the adult equivalent. When I taught my own boys to read they were paid a penny a page for their labours, though the rate later went up to twopence with the increased cost of living. Each penny they earned was marked with a stroke in the back of the book, and the system had the added advantage of teaching them to count. By the time Deborah came to learn the system was more elaborate. I kept a basket of small prizes which were priced (rather unrealistically) with tickets ranging from a penny to sixpence. She would then spend her earnings at the 'shop', and knew all there was to know about the value of sixpence before she had finished.

In school too I kept a basket of prizes - not priced, but to be dished out on special occasions such as reaching the end of a reader. Later when the work became more diversified I instituted a system of stars. Each child had a pink card on which I stuck silver stars for good work in any field. Ten stars added up to a cloud (heaven knows where the terminology came from) which merited a prize. At the end of the term the one with the most stars was awarded the 'star badge', a much coveted prize, for the best work of the term. This system meant that the youngest had an equal chance with the oldest to earn stars, because they were awarded for success by the child's own standards. In practice the star badge went to the child who had made the most progress during the term, not the cleverest. We did not have bad marks - I always find that positive encouragement works better - though on one or two occasions I cancelled stars which were discovered to have been obtained by false pretences - that is, copying the answers from someone else. I always dinned it into the children that what mattered to each of them was their own individual progress, no matter what anyone else may be doing. They must master each step for themselves, and the fact that the next child was quicker or slower than they were was entirely irrelevant. This was one advantage of the age-spread; because they were of different ages it was accepted that they would be at different stages. This eliminated competition; the slower children had always someone in the group who was behind them, except the youngest, who expected to be behind and were pleased to have got as far as they had. I never awarded marks, so that there could be no odious comparisons - just stars for good work. Mistakes were taken as evidence that the work was not yet fully understood; we went over the point again and the mistakes were corrected, but no one was ever shamed for not understanding.

Writing developed naturally from the writing-patterns and pictures, though as I taught them each separate letter I took care that they formed it in a certain way, establishing motor habits that would ensure the smoothest possible transition to a good cursive hand later. Taking a tip from Maria Montessori I cut sets of letters out of sandpaper and mounted them individually on cards. Children who found it difficult to memorise the shape of a letter visually were often quick to learn by 'feel' with closed eyes: this went for numbers too. For practice in making the letters we had individual blackboards and coloured chalks - these were highly popular, especially when it came to the rubbing-out part.

Every day began with the 'news' session, when each child in turn held the floor for a few minutes and imparted his juiciest bits of information to the rest of us. I always found this highly entertaining, and acquired an intimate knowledge of the private lives of all their families which they would have found somewhat disconcerting had they known. Everyone then illustrated some aspect of his 'news' in a special book and dictated a caption for me to inscribe below. Then they would copy the caption, and soon I wrote it on a separate piece of paper for them to copy into the book. Finally they would write their own caption on paper for me to check the spelling before copying it in. Simple word cards were available for them to look up words they did not know.

We made endless picture books, both individually and class efforts, labelled first with simple words, then with sentences. The next stage was story books, a sort of strip-cartoon with captions, and soon the children were taking their first steps in the free writing which was to become such a major aspect of our work. Once they gained the urge to write they were quite carried away by the possibilities that their new skill opened up to them. I just let them write as much as they wanted to without discouraging them by overmuch correction of spelling and punctuation; this came later. The result was some quite extraordinary imaginative writing and poetry, and in the long run their spelling and punctuation certainly did not suffer for it.

As soon as they could read a little they were given 'work-books'. These have lots of pictures to colour according to simple instructions, words to fill in, puzzles to do, and involve easy reading and counting and writing. We stocked a large variety of them and the children loved them. It meant that they always had something enjoyable and instructive to get on with, and never had to sit around getting bored when I was busy with someone else. Also it formed in them the habit of getting on with their own work without constant prodding and assistance, a habit which was essential to the way we worked later on.

During that first year we did hardly any formal number work, but we spent many hours with apparatus of all sorts (most of it home-made) becoming absolutely familiar with the numbers up to ten - odd and even numbers, counting forwards and backwards, counting in twos and threes, learning the pairs of numbers that add up to ten; in concrete terms only we learned the meaning of addition and subtraction, multiplication and division with reference to numbers up to ten. They also learned to write the numbers and to count up to a hundred. The only written work consisted of filling in 'counting books', which have lots of pictures of groups of objects beside which you write the appropriate figure. There was also a great deal of water and sand play, pouring quantities from one jug to a smaller or larger one, to give meaning to the term 'volume', and of weighing many different commodities. There were no 'sums' at all, but I still think that they learned more basic maths in that year than they will ever learn in a year again.

Deborah had done all this earlier, being a little older, so she did go on to sums, and romped gaily through the prescribed course for children up to the age of seven in the first two terms - which just shows that once you have mastered the numbers up to ten the rest is chickenfeed. The mysterious 'tens and units' were explained with the help of some coloured plastic cocktail sticks and some rubber bands. You put a random heap of sticks on the table, count them into bundles of ten, and secure each bundle with a band. What you have left over are units. When it comes to adding several double-figure numbers together there is no problem - if you get more than ten units you simple put a band round them and add them to the tens pile. Similarly with subtraction - if you do not have enough units to subtract the required number, you just undo a 'bundle of ten' and take what you need from that. Long after the sticks were no longer used, the children visualised the concrete operation and talked about 'undoing bundles of ten'. Years later when Deborah went to a school where they used the method of complementary addition she was completely mystified - it seemed unnecessary and illogical, and very confusing.

At this time the older ones spent about half their time on the three Rs, including the considerable amount of time taken up by the stories and poems which I read to them each day. By now I was cautiously introducing the traditional folk myths; I had a collection of large bright pictures to illustrate these, but I always told the stories, never read them. This way I could edit out all the nasty bits - we all enjoyed them much better that way. I was surprised to discover that there exists a school of thought among professional nursery teachers which maintains that small children should be told the traditional fairy tales in all their terrifying detail (as written up by the Grimm brothers and Hans Andersen); the theory is that children entertain such evil thoughts themselves that it comforts them to discover that they are not abnormal, that other people are evil too - contrary to the impression they receive from the superficially civilised world around them. Though there may be something in this from the psychological point of view (not being a psychologist I wouldn't know), it seems to me that in the first place children should not be encouraged to think of their own evil impulses as normal; after all, the world they move in is civilised as far as they are concerned, and though evil undoubtedly does exist in the world at large they are unlikely to come into contact with it until they are much older and better able to cope with it. Secondly anyone who has seen terror in the eyes of an imaginative three year old listening to tales of someone's Grandma being eaten by a wolf, or of children being left in the forest to starve by their own parents, would not think that the price was worth the doubtful psychological returns. Perhaps there are some unimaginative children who take these horror stories quite calmly, not having grasped what they are really about; moreover at a later stage many children, particularly boys, enjoy death and violence at second hand as a sort of game, as in cowboy films. 'Dead' does not mean anything more than falling to the ground (and, understood, getting up again afterwards). This stage is not reached before the age of five at least, usually nearer seven, so what possible justification there can be for teaching young nursery nurses to dish out horror stories to the under-fives is difficult to understand.

Quite apart from the element of fear, the moral standards of the traditional heroes are often directly opposed to those that we try to instill into our children. Jack, of beanstalk fame, was nothing less than a thief and a thug by modern standards; Puss-in-Boots and his master mere con-men; even Hansel and Gretel committed murder in the furtherance of theft; and the children are not slow to point out these moral discrepancies. On the other hand the traditional tales do have a charm which appeals greatly to children, harking back as they do to a simple, picturesque, and apparently carefree peasant existence in contrast to the pressures and privations that modern living exerts even on the children.

On the whole we avoided 'Little Red Riding Hood', 'Hansel and Gretel', and 'Jack and the Beanstalk' until they were six, or even older. 'The Three Bears' went down much better, and 'The Ginger-bread Man' (though they were always very shocked that he was eaten in the end). 'The Three Little Pigs' had to be suitably edited too - we glossed over the fate of the first two little pigs, and the wolf was finally dispatched in a much more humane manner.

Even such old favourites as 'Little Black Sambo' can be frightening if read straight. From long practice I knew it by heart, so I recited it with suitable actions to soften the edges a bit, and add the touch of humour that the pictures lack to the literal-minded child. I am told that this story has now been banned in some schools because of its racial connotations; which I think is misguided when I remember a little African girl in a five-year-old class I once taught. When she heard the story for the first time her face wreathed in smiles and she commented happily, 'He's just like me - not like any of you, but just like me.' I think she got fed up with these endless stories about white children, and this was the first one she could identify with.

The Beatrix Potter books were always much loved and never frightening, apart from 'Samuel Whiskers', where Tom Kitten is made up into a roly-poly pudding by those detestable rats and only rescued from a nasty death in the nick of time - it terrified the daylights out of me as a child.

A. A. Milne was popular too, both Pooh and the poems, and some of R. L. Stevenson's poetry for children. In fact there is never any difficulty in finding things to read to young children - the only problem lies in the choice among so much that is delectable; and the only restriction lies in their conservatism - they want to hear their favourites over and over again.

The second half of the morning was divided between painting and 'making', free play, and music. Because music is one of my chief joys in life, it became an integral part of our school life too. For a time we followed the BBC 'Music and Movement' programme, but soon got bored with it; it lacked inspiration, we felt, was too restrained, and was always so much the same. We preferred our own free interpretation of music. This was becoming more lively and imaginative as they got older, drawing as they did upon a wider range of experience and ideas. Their dancing gave form to what was before a confused image in their minds, and was in turn reflected in their painting and their play. Stories and pictures of wild animals, and most of all television programmes, gave new meaning to the old jungle record; there was much discussion on how tigers and elephants and monkeys move and behave, and then a rash of paintings showing with vivid simplicity these animals really moving. That was the great difference that the dancing made - their paintings depicted movement, which is unusual in children's pictures, whose figures tend to be wooden and static.

One day bongoes were mentioned in a television programme, which led to experiments with old tins, sheet rubber, and broad adhesive tape. From this we went on to home-made maraccas, bells, and tap-boxes, and even castanets, which involved much more complicated woodwork than we had tackled hitherto. These were used to accompany songs and records with much more zest and accuracy than the orthodox percussion instruments had ever inspired. Then someone noticed that so far we were only able to play rhythms, not tunes, which sparked off an inquiry into pitched instruments. We tried rubber bands, combs and tissue paper, and finally jam-jars of water which we tuned pretty accurately to the diatonic scale. By now they all wanted to know about orchestral instruments; I dug out all the relevant pictures and books I could find, revealed the insides of the piano, and produced a recorder, but these only whetted their appetite. We had one or two records that identified the sounds of various instruments, and 'Peter and the Wolf' gave much material for listening, acting, painting and drawing, but what we really needed was to see a real live orchestra in action.

A concert seemed out of the question, but soon the problem was solved by the visit to the local theatre of the Royal Ballet. Why not take the children to see this? The idea would not have occurred to me but for the chance remark of a friend that she had taken her four-year-old son to the ballet and he had been spellbound. So I took a block booking for the matinee performance of 'The Nutcracker'. Before we went I produced a book with the story and pictures of the ballet so that the children would know what to expect, and it was such a huge success that the ballet became a regular twice-yearly fixture as long as the school lasted. During the interval the children rushed down to the orchestra pit and made friends with the drummer before he had time to disappear through the hatch. He stayed and showed them everything, rather surprised at their keen interest. Some of the youngest children found the programme a bit long and were restless, and the boys were not as wildly enthusiastic as the girls in later years, but there was no doubt that it made a tremendous impression on them. For long afterwards the story and characters were reflected in their play, their painting, their dancing.

Throughout the early years of the nursery school I had tried in vain to find someone to come and play the piano. I could play only enough to pick out a tune and had to rely on my voice and records for everything else. But at last we found Mary, whom the children always called simply Mrs Hab because they could not pronounce her surname, and she brought a new dimension to the life of the school. To begin with she patiently taught them to sing sweetly and in tune - young children singing are usually far from pleasant to listen to, but after a term or two these were an exception. She introduced them to some of the loveliest of the traditional songs as well as gems that few people have ever heard before. We strictly avoided anything labelled 'Songs for Little Children' because the music, striving so hard after simplicity, was always so poor as to be not worth the trouble of learning: except in the case of certain children's hymns, usually taken from 'Songs of Praise'. Another of Mary's (many) gifts was that she could play anything to order on the piano, and together we evolved our own 'music and movement' programmes that were far more fun than the BBC variety.

At this time the older children were beginning to lose interest in painting except when something really fired their imagination - or as a release from some sort of tension. In other words they ceased to use it as a regular form of communication and reserved it for the occasions when words failed them. I once read that the colours children use bear a direct relation to their emotional state; I dismissed it as unlikely at the time, but revised my opinion as I watched children paint, particularly the very young children. Mentally disturbed, or just angry and frustrated children, dashed off sinister daubs in black, red, purple, or dark brown; when they were happy and carefree they used bright colours and white, and painted with much more care. Frightened children externalised their fears by painting pictures about them. Deborah broke her leg when she was small and spent a brief but terrifying time in hospital; for months afterwards she painted vivid pictures of death and disaster involving ambulances, nurses, doctors with masks, and people being wheeled on trolleys. A little boy who had seen a house on fire painted terrifying pictures of burning houses with people inside.

Colours in themselves fascinated the children too. As well as the ready-mixed paints I sometimes gave them dry powder colours to mix for themselves. We explored various new techniques such as printing (with sticks, potatoes, leaves, or anything else that came to hand), spatter painting and marbling. New possibilities became apparent too with the big wax crayons - wax resist, 'invisible' painting, etching on layers of wax, or combining wax with colour wash or ink or charcoal. We experimented with everything we could think of.

When it came to making Christmas presents I tried hard to think up something that would be genuinely of use, and yet would be within the capabilities of such young children - where they would have some chance of achieving a good effect. However well the parents may react to some of the unrecognisable monstrosities that their children bring home from school, I do not believe that the children themselves get any real satisfaction from them. In the end I settled for three or four simple items - tubes of sweets wrapped in crepe paper to look like crackers, felt needlebooks (the pieces cut out with pinking shears) which some of their grandmothers are still using, woolly balls tied on to a teething ring for the baby, woolly men as car-mascots or fixed on to a pin as a brooch for little sisters. The sweet-crackers were a great test of unselfishness - it was a miracle if any of them reached their intended recipients.

I loathe paper chains - we always thought up our own Christmas decorations. During our autumn walks we used to collect larch cones and put them by for December, when we would paint them white and gold and strew them along the shelves and windowsills. We saved a few to stick round the red candles stuck into bases of plaster of Paris. Early in December we set off to the woods, armed with secateurs, to gather holly and ivy, yew and fir. We loved the woods in all their moods, but there was always a particular excitement about this trip. We knew just where to find what we wanted; eager eyes sought out the brightest berries, the greenest branches, and busy hands, regardless of cold and scratches, clipped and twisted them from the reluctant trees. Then home we bore our spoil in triumph, to range it along the beams and ledges. We filled big stone jars with yew and studded it with tiny silver bells, and made a green bower to shelter Mary and Joseph, the baby, the shepherds, and the kings. The children cut out lacey white snow-flakes and stuck them on to red foil; these, suspended on fine thread from the beams, turned in the warm air and sparkled with reflected light. The heady smell of pine filled the room; the festive greenery, the red candles, the gold, and the miriad pin-pricks of shining light, like stars, all combined to transform the familiar schoolroom into a place of mystery and excitement, the very essence of Christmas.

When the children were older they made their own crib, with foot-high figures - wire-based and dressed magnificently from the scrap-basket. We always had a wonderful collection of bits of material - all the families contributed the cuttings from their dressmaking, which must have included not a few very glamorous evening dresses.

Our interest in nature that year centred on four rabbits who had taken up residence in the yard. These rabbits destroyed many of my illusions; I had bought them naïvely thinking that they would be mild and gentle creatures, suitable pets for little children, but I might as well have imported a nest of rats. The minute I put them all to feed together in the new run they flew at each others' throats and would have done murder if I had not rushed to separate them - getting bitten and lacerated for my pains. After that they were kept strictly separated in pairs - it was only by trial and error that I discovered what sex they all were. Apparently the only way to stop them killing each other was to put one pair in each of the only two hutches, and after that, despite their extreme youth, they presented us with two new litters roughly every six weeks. They had some educational value in that the children soon knew all there was to know about mating and reproduction; a few tactfully-phrased questions from them led to open class discussion of this fascinating subject, and elucidation of the mystery once and for all. After this there were no tabu subjects in school - anything that came up was discussed freely and unemotionally, and we seemed to avoid altogether the 'lavatory humour' stage, unless it came up much later when they went into bigger schools.

Only one of the rabbits was at all likable; his name was Thumper, and he had a curious habit of chewing his way out of the hutch and taking his exercise on the roof. He got up there by a series of leaps from bench to dustbin to lower roof, and then up to the steeply-pitched house roof. Once up there he took a lot of enticing down; we would plead and bribe from the yard while he sat up unconcernedly on the ridge sniffing the morning air, eyeing us out of his eye-corner until the bribe became interesting enough to consider.

As with all the pets the children were interested in them for a time and overfed them vastly, but eventually they lost interest and forgot all about them. Then I thankfully gave them away because they took a lot of looking after. They took much more interest in the endless collection of wildlife which they kept in the classroom. At various times we had worms in darkened jars (to watch them making tunnels), beetles of all sorts, caterpillars and butterflies, a queen wasp, annual colonies of tadpoles, frogs and toads, minnows and pond life of all sorts, not to mention dead bats and moles, birds' nests and eggs; we once bred hundreds of water snails in a few months from one original that we found in some watercress - this puzzled them until I explained how, and led to an interesting side-line study of hermaphrodites. We hatched snails' eggs and spiders' eggs; on one exciting occasion we thought that we had caught a colorado beetle and reported it hopefully to the police (there was a public hunt on for them at the time because of a particular threat to crops); a policeman was solemnly sent along to examine it, but after some research it turned out to be something else, so we just kept it for a pet for a bit.

Because the yard was not much of a stamping ground for energetic four and five year olds we tried to do something by way of exercise most afternoons. There was as yet no official afternoon school and the smaller children found the mornings enough, but usually some of the mothers helped to entertain the older ones in the afternoons. Our walks took us all over the countryside as well as the town. We always carried a little trug with us for the children's treasures, and examined these in school at leisure the next day. In the autumn we went blackberrying, and took a picnic tea to eat afterwards in the warm mellow sunshine. We gathered armloads of hips and haws too and brought them back to arrange against a background of evergreen in the big stone jars. Even when school became an all-day affair these walks remained a regular feature of school life. One of the chief sins of ordinary school is that it shuts children up when they should be out of doors with the sun and the wind in their hair, and the freedom to stretch their young limbs as nature intended. We never did much in the way of formal nature study, but we learned a lot by just being in the country, and looking and watching and collecting things.

The birds that came to feed on the windowsill in winter provided us with considerable interest. On the wall beside the window were pictures of all the ones that came regularly, so that everyone was soon able to identify them. Then we began to notice what each kind liked to eat from the variety of food that we offered them, so that we could classify them as seed-eaters or insect-eaters, and from that noticed the shape of the beak. Some children made their own 'bird books', and this led to an interest in birds farther afield, so that bird-spotting became a habit on our walks.

Nicky as he grew older became our expert naturalist. He was remarkably knowledgeable about animals and flowers, and later fossils became his passion - he used to go quite far afield to collect them with his father and brought fascinating samples to school. When he was very small he once took me all round a flower bed in a little park where we happened to be killing some time together, and touching each flower with surprising delicacy explained what each one was. On our school walks we were passionate collectors of wild flowers, and Nicky could usually be relied upon to identify them. One day someone rushed up to me with some lacey white flower and asked me what it was, and without looking too closely (I was talking to someone) I said, 'Cow parsley.' Nicky, aged five, looked up in surprise: 'It couldn't be cow-parsley, could it,' he said gently. 'Look at the leaves.' He was quite right of course, it couldn't possibly.

One afternoon a week we used to go swimming in an indoor teaching pool at a nearby primary school, where there were two instructresses who were experts at getting small children waterborne. The little girls loved the water and seemed quite unafraid, but the boys at this age were terrified and we just had to stop taking them after a bit - though by the age of six or thereabouts they were as confident in the water as anybody. My chief memory of these trips is of Rebecca and Isobel sitting in the water as though in armchairs and rotating with supreme dignity and contentment; they were both the same age (three) and very much the same build - chubby and rosy and placid, and they took their pleasures seriously. For a long time they were the youngest in the group - a position that they did not always relish - but they were determined to keep up with the others and would not be left out of anything.

We did not have any formal physical training lessons because the children seemed to get all the exercise that they needed naturally, but at one stage this worried one of the fathers (a doctor), so we advertised for a professional gymnast to come once or twice a week to oversee the children's physical development - and Mrs Tubb turned up. She was young and muscular with a gleam in her eye that I should have recognised as fanatical. She was apparently used to exerting a tougher discipline on her class than ours were prepared to accept, or else she thought that she was dealing with an army PT course. She became known as Sergeant-major Tubb and the children took an intense dislike to her - which in itself was disturbing, because as a rule they welcomed any new adult with a friendly interest which frequently blossomed into heart-warming affection. Having employed her as the expert I was reluctant to interfere, but after tears and protests from the children I thought I had better go and see what was happening. I found her forcing their young limbs into positions nature never intended, which brought tears to their eyes and cries of agony to their lips. I tried doing some of these exercises myself and understood why. Afterwards I suggested that they were perhaps a little young for such formal gymnastics and that what I had in mind was something a little less rigorous, but the sergeant-major assured me earnestly that these exercises were possible and that it was just a case of discipline! After that we decided to rely on our own resources to keep ourselves healthy, and I can't say that I ever noticed any serious deformities or lack of suppleness.

One highly successful outing that year was a visit to the farm to watch the milking. It all began when someone evinced a great interest in cows, and a reluctance to believe that the milk one drank for breakfast was somehow produced by them. There were various strange theories about the actual mechanics of this, so I thought they had better go and see for themselves. It was a modern dairy with electric milking machines, and the cowman was a friendly man. We stood in a long row behind the cows and watched everything in silence, and then gazed up at the shining pipes that carried the milk to the dairy for cooling. The cowman offered us mugs of the new milk to drink, but on the whole we preferred ours older, pasteurised and refrigerated. We did however bring some of it home to make cream-cheese with - you can't make proper cream-cheese with this new-fangled homogenised stuff. I thought, from the utter lack of comment, that the children were perhaps too young to have understood what they had seen, but I changed my mind the next morning when they set to work to build a model of the milkfarm in school. There it was in every detail - a cow in each stall, string (carefully frayed into four strands at one end) clamped on to its undercarriage with Plasticine; the string led to overhead pipes (straws) which in turn led to the cooler, a convincing replica made of silver paper. There were bulls and calves in the fields outside, and a tanker waiting to transport the milk to the bottling factory down the road. Farther along was a row of houses and a milk-float, and outside each house one or two minute bottles of milk with red tops, made of 'glitter-wax'. All this took a week to finish, and meanwhile we made cream-cheese and invited the parents to a cheese-tasting party. The whole project had involved a lot of writing of explanatory labels, reading, drawing, handwork - and of course a lot of fun.

At the end of the week someone decided that the poor cows had been clamped to the milking machines long enough and ventured to return them to pasture. This brought forth an irritated bellow from someone else: 'Who's put the brown cow with the black bull?' Then followed a fierce argument on genetics that would have indeed startled some of their parents.

CHAPTER 5

Freedom to Explore

The following September we settled down for the first time as just ourselves. The nursery school had finally been wound up and Margaret had gone off to another job - she was after all a nursery nurse, not a school-teacher. Rebecca, Isobel, Nicky and Sebbie joined us in the schoolroom and watched with big eyes everything that the older ones did. Since this is essentially the children's story perhaps this is the place to introduce them more personally. This I find quite the most difficult task of all, to give a picture of each one that will make their story come alive without embarrassing them. I have no doubt that they will read my account with a critical eye, hence the egg-shell delicacy of my assignment.

First then the two oldest, Candy and Deborah, completely different in both looks and temperament. Candy, slim and graceful with long fair hair, was the dreamer of the class. Unacademic, she was perhaps the least in tune with the enthusiasms of the book-lovers, but she was highly imaginative and for much of the time lost in a dream-world of her own. She was in her element in the dancing and dramatic activities - anything that demanded dramatic interpretation.

In contrast Deborah, dark-haired and dark-eyed, was vivacious, enthusiastic, impatient to try out her inexhaustible fund of ideas and organise the others as supporting cast.

Jose, sturdy and cheerful, with a deep voice and clear grey

eyes, was an uncomplicated character who threw herself wholeheartedly into whatever was afoot. She was primarily an outdoor child, tanned and athletic; despite a contempt for unnecessary wrappings, even in winter she was hardly ever ill - it was a rash bug that dared to attack Jo!

Graham was shy, gentle, sensitive; when he first came he did not speak to me at all (or to anyone else for that matter) for the whole of his first term, but when he did finally manage to communicate, his conversation was well worth listening to. He found physical co-ordination an effort when he was little, but what he lacked in manual skill he made up for intellectually; he had a good head for figures.

Michela was neat, self-possessed, and a born organiser; with her fair hair, even features and fresh complexion, she was nearly always dressed in white and light colours, and yet always managed to look clean and tidy - I don't know how she did it; Candy and Clare seemed to have this gift too, but all the others just attracted grime naturally. Serene and capable, she always took charge in a crisis.

Clare, the youngest in her family like Rebecca, never embraced school with such whole-hearted enthusiasm as the others did; she always cast wistful glances homeward. A bright-eyed sturdy child, she watched with interest the activities of the others while maintaining a certain reserve herself.

Catherine, tiny, with curling hair and dancing eyes, had all the energy and lively curiosity that stamped the children reared in our own nursery. She was an avid reader from an early age, but it was through her hands that she best revealed herself, in writing and drawings of painstaking neatness and precision; she knew exactly what she wanted to put on to paper and was determined to finish it in her own time and in her own way.

These seven formed the older half of the group and for convenience were known collectively as the 'Biggies' in our own private parlance. The younger half included the four who had just joined us in the schoolroom, then Elwyn, who was the youngest of the group, and for the last year or so Antonia and Edward.

Rebecca had been in the school in one way or another since she was six months old. At first she participated from her pram in the yard, where the other children would push her furiously up and down, every now and again letting go of the pram so that it would crash into the back gate - fortunately she never got hurt and regarded it as a huge joke. Later she stayed with Margaret in the Baby nursery while I looked after the bigger ones, but this distressed her considerably - she always wanted to be with me, if possible in what she claimed as her rightful position, on my lap. I might be teacher to all the others but as far as she was concerned I was simply 'Mummie'. As she grew older her chief delight lay in painting and music, particularly the dancing; both she and Candy responded to music with a sensitivity and grace delightful to watch.

The first time I met Sebbie he was wearing a blue pram suit, but what I remember were the huge eyes alight with happiness and laughter that shone out from amid the blue. He grew up small, wiry, and bubbling over with mischief and energy; his ready humour prevented us from ever taking ourselves too seriously. His chief talents lay in an unusually good grasp of number, and a facility for composing limericks.

Nicky was tolerant, good-natured, and placid. Though surprisingly knowledgeable about things that interested him he remained unflustered by the enthusiasm of the others when it came to the 3 Rs.

Isobel on the other hand was determined to get ahead and catch up with the big ones, and she worked very hard to that end. Blue-eyed and curly-haired, with a contented chuckle, she threw herself into everything with a will and refused firmly to be left out of anything.

Elwyn joined us the minute she was old enough to do so without disrupting the rest of the group - she had her foot in the door from the moment she could walk. Small and passionate, with an extraordinary dynamism, we called her our 'atomic bomb'. She was a natural gymnast, fearless, and strong beyond expectation. When she was very small she had bursts of absolutely uncontrollable fury, when those who knew her simply got out of her way until she cooled down, but apart from these lapses her utter charm and her uninhibited affection were irresistible. She had long fair hair and big blue eyes alight with interest, and she embraced all our activities with tremendous zest and enjoyment. At the age of four she could read, and she wrote long involved stories complete with lively illustrations.

Antonia was only with us for the last year and a half; when she came at the age of five she could read and write fluently and spent a lot of her time writing highly imaginative stories and poems. She had a great feel for language and a love of words for their own sake, but she scorned maths - having little or no groundwork in number she always found this side of our work difficult and there was not time enough to make good the deficiency. Small and dark, determined and intelligent, she would grumble and scold volubly when she thought too much was being demanded of her: 'I'm only little,' she would assert firmly - she must have found it rather exhausting being thrown suddenly into a company as exuberant as ours. She was held in affection and some amusement by the others, and rather mothered as the 'youngest member' (though literally she wasn't).

Edward came too late to be much influenced by the group; emotionally very much younger than all the others, he stayed on the edge and watched our antics with some bewilderment.

For four or five years twelve of these children lived together in such a close relationship that they had all the ease and familiarity of siblings. There was a certain amount of quarrelling as in any family, but there was a lack of tension and reserve between them that enabled them to develop naturally and happily.

The old Baby nursery was now renamed the 'Bookroom'; it made a delightful quiet reading-room, and we were glad to have more room for the books which were by now piling up considerably. The biggest slice of our budget went on these, and by the time the school closed we had a class library of over a thousand books, all chosen for their attractiveness as well as their value as good stories or for their information.

The timetable changed too. Most of the children were five now and ready for full-day school, so we laid on lunch and school went on until three o'clock. The little ones still only stayed for the morning, but they soon were clamouring to stay for the afternoon too - they hated to miss anything.

The question of lunch was to become one of our biggest headaches. At first my housekeeper cooked it, but she had soon had enough of us all and sailed off like Dr Dolittle's sister in search of a tidier and more tranquil existence - though in her case it was not mice in the piano but just too many children!

After that I cooked it, but it was impossible to shop, cook, and wash up afterwards at the same time as giving the children all the attention they needed.

Next we tried a professional caterer. The food was delivered from the kitchens of a nearby restaurant, but it was so nasty (albeit expensive) that only the hardiest could stomach it. When Clare, who was normally a co-operative child, declared open rebellion and refused to stay at school for lunch, and I found Candy's lunches for the past week quietly mouldering in her apron pocket, I recognised defeat and agreed that we would have to make other arrangements.

There were no other restaurants nearby, and the cost of employing someone just to shop, cook, and clear away lunches for so few people, would have priced the meals beyond all reason. In desperation I called on the supervisor of the local authority schools' meals service and tried to persuade her to drop us off a cannister or two of food on their rounds, but apparently this was impossible.

Meanwhile we improvised. As soon as morning school was over I sped down to the kitchen to light the gas under a large pan of soup, and while the children cleared up the schoolroom and washed down the tables I ran across the road to buy fresh wholemeal rolls. To this we added cold meat, cheese, salad and fruit, and for a time managed well enough, though it got rather monotonous in the winter. Even with this arrangement there was the problem of shopping for the fruit and salad every day or so - the mothers helped, but it was difficult to arrange a reliable rota.

Eventually the mothers came to our rescue and took it in turns to carry the children off each day to lunch in their homes, but in the end even this system broke down owing to the simultaneous arrival of several new babies; so we reverted to cold lunches once more, each child bringing his own picnic, and this seemed the only satisfactory solution to the problem.

Practically all the older children could read fluently by this time - to the great surprise of the HMI when he came. I was amused to hear him say to someone:

'And can you read?'

'Yes' - in surprised tones.

'Would you like to read me some of this book?'

'All right.' The child looked at him rather curiously, wondering whether perhaps he could not read it himself. Followed a passage fluently read, interrupted by a hasty 'Oh yes, I see you can. Can you read too?'

'Of course I can' - rather indignantly. Proof followed.

'And how old are you?'

'Four' - and so on. It just happened that everyone there could read and were rather surprised and insulted that the man should have doubted it.

Then he went on to look at their workbooks. He leaned over Jose's shoulder as she wrote.

'And are you going to put "Ding-dong-bell" (or whatever it was) there?' he asked.

'Don't be silly, of course not,' replied Jose with a fruity chuckle at the man's stupidity - he obviously had not taken time to read the instructions properly. After a bit the HMI came to me looking worried.

'They should not work all the time at this age,' he said. 'They need to paint and do hand-work and so on - you do give them some time to play, don't you.'

I assured him that we did indeed do all these things - in fact I thought it impolitic to admit just how little time we did spend on what might be termed 'work'. At that time probably not more than one hour a day was spent on formal reading, writing and arithmetic - all the rest of the time went on making things, playing, listening to stories, just talking (this took up a vast amount of time), and pottering round the countryside - plus singing and dancing, listening to and making music, swimming, and so on.

It has always seemed to me that there is something wrong with the organisation when schools have to keep young children sitting dully at desks for long hours a day and still take years to teach them to read and write. In our school we confined our mechanical learning to short intensive periods, but during these the children were quiet and really did concentrate - and covered the ground remarkably quickly. Their powers of concentration were unusual, and I like to think that it had something to do with the early nursery training - quiet application to a jigsaw puzzle until it was completed, and so on. This characteristic was certainly confined to the children who had been through our own nursery; the others accepted the same working habits as the rest but could not concentrate for so long.

Now that the children could read, the real fun of learning could begin, although we still spent a brief period each morning on the sheer mechanics of reading and writing (phonetics and word-building, spelling, writing-practice, and so on). For the rest I just let them loose on the largest and most exciting collection of books that I could muster and waited to see what would emerge. All sorts of things did, and developed in the most exciting way.

One day Deborah erupted into the room muffled up in anorak, gloves and trousers, with small plastic tennis racquets tied on to her booted feet.

'Who am I?' she demanded. The others looked up with interest.

'Captain Scott,' replied someone with certainty. Most of them had read the Ladybird book about Captain Scott, and those who had not hastily did so in order to be in on the latest interest. Arguments raged about how Amundsen got to the Pole first, about whether it was quite cricket for him to have done so, and just what Scott and his men must have felt like when they realised that they had been forestalled. I produced all the books and pictures I could find about the Polar regions generally, told them about other explorers, and about the contemporary teams still researching there. We had Eskimo stories, learned about huskies and seals, penguins and polar bears; drew pictures and made books and wrote stories until we were thoroughly immersed in the subject. Then one day we went to London and visited Scott's ship the *Discovery*, moored on the Embankment. The children were thrilled to see Scott's own writing in the log-book, and the names of his companions over the cabin doors. They were surprised at the smallness of the ship, and thought how terrifying and uncomfortable it must have been in rough Antarctic waters among the pack-ice. The sailor in charge was amused at their eager interest, but rather taken aback when one of them said in a puzzled voice:

'But where is Oates' cabin, and Captain Evans'? They aren't here.'

The mystery was explained by the fact that the *Discovery* was used on an earlier voyage; on the last fatal trip, when Oates and Evans had indeed been with Scott, they had taken another ship, the *Terra Nova*. The sailor told us that on his last trip Scott had tried to get the *Discovery* again because he regarded it as a lucky ship, but it was not available.

These trips became an integral part of our school life. Because we were free and manœuvrable we could go at a day's notice to see whatever fitted in with the interest of the moment. If we needed transport the parents provided it in cars; or if we were bound farther afield and were going by train they would dutifully deliver their children to the station in time for the early morning train - equipped only with a mackintosh and money for fares and food. On these occasions I brought a basket containing packets of (unsickly, non-sticky) sweets, comics, a damp face-flannel and a comb - necessary for cleaning the children up at the end of the day before their mothers saw them - packets of paper handkerchiefs, a notebook and pencil per child, and a communal packet of crayons.

We were used to travelling about and everyone knew the drill. They settled down at once in the train to read their comics or draw in the notebooks - jumping around the compartment making a noise was definitely 'not done'. In the street they formed a crocodile, two and two, with the two oldest and most reliable pairs fore and aft - the one to lead and make sure they stopped the whole line at the road-crossings, the other to act as whippers-in to make sure that nobody got lost. The youngest ones and the slowest walkers were firmly sandwiched in the middle. Like this we moved rapidly around the streets, in and out of London traffic, on and off buses and underground trains, up and down escalators; though these last sometimes proved rather a problem as some of the children were too young to get on and off by themselves. I used to feed them all on one at a time at the bottom, then race all the way up to the top in time to disembark the first in line.

Often one or other of the mothers came with me on these trips. The trouble was when lots of parents decided to come; then it was chaotic. They would wander in all directions with unknown numbers of children and I was terrified that we would lose one. I spent the day like an anxious collie trying to round up my flock.

Meals we usually bought at a cafeteria and the children

were old hands at queuing up with their trays, ordering their own meal and paying for it at the other end. One day, after sailing up the Thames to Greenwich, we queued up at an East End fish and chip shop and ate our one-and sixpenn'orth out of newspaper, duly sprinkled with salt and vinegar in the approved style. This was a new experience for the children and they lapped it up with relish. As an occasional treat when returning from a day in London we had tea on the train. Then I confined my attentions to the youngest fry and left the older ones to do their own ordering - though I was startled to hear Catherine, when asked by the waiter what she would like, reply in a lordly voice: 'I think I'll have wine to-day.'

Much of our project work centred on historical topics, though I don't remember that we ever called it that. In addition to her musical talents Mrs Hab is by trade a historian, and she now came one afternoon a week to develop this side of things. Not that we aimed at teaching a lot of battles and dates, but the children were already showing an interest in other times and customs and we wanted to give them a broad general outline of events and periods - a framework on which they could later hang more detailed studies. What Mrs Hab taught them in the afternoons I developed in morning school.

We had already come across the Romans when talking about the background to stories of Jesus, and had been intrigued by a very fine model of a Roman villa in the museum. We visited too the Roman villa at Chedworth, in Gloucestershire, which brought the period to life as nothing else had done. I read them, in translation, Tacitus' description of Britain at the time of the Roman invasion, and that led us on, after stopping to admire Caratacus and Boadicea, to look at pictures of Hadrian's Wall, and one or two of the older ones enjoyed Kipling's stories of the Centurion on the Wall in 'Puck of Pook's Hill'.

This brought us on to our own beginnings and so to cavemen. I read them Lucy Fitch Perkins' 'The Cave Twins', which they loved, after which they made a model, in papier mâché, of a cave under a hillside; there were shaggy brown figures (papier mâché on a wire base) roasting some animal over a fire, primitive weapons and tools lying about, and on the hill a superb mammoth, again papier mâché on wire, created by Jose. We went searching for flints on the Downs (and proudly brought back several), made primitive clay pots with pointed bases like we had seen at the museum, and clay models of stone oil lamps to see how they worked. We made arrowheads like the real ones we had collected and lashed them to wooden shafts with strips of thonging, just to find out what the technical problems would be - we found there were plenty.

Later we got on to Saxon times and built a very elaborate model of a Saxon village, complete in every detail as far as we could make it from the reference books we had. One morning we had a visitor (we had a lot of visitors who tended to add interest one way or another); this one turned out to be a historian and knew all about Saxon times, it seemed. He admired the model, but asked:

'Where are the pigs? Every Saxon village would have had pigs, and a swineherd, and an oak-wood with acorns for the pigs to eat,' and he went on to tell us a lot we didn't know about the Saxons and to suggest other improvements to the model, all of which were effected with great enthusiasm. By this time our modelling technique had been improved by the use of balsa wood, cut on a board with craft-knives; this made things like fencing and rustic bridges possible and gave us much more realistic effects.

William the Conqueror and the Battle of Hastings gave us material for a lot of happy activity. Mrs Hab had brought a book about the Bayeux tapestry to give the children some idea of what the costumes of the day and the Norman armour looked like, and this inspired one of our most treasured possessions, our own Bayeux tapestry. On another afternoon each week Jose's mother Rachel came to sew with the children. They had just finished making stuffed animals and were wondering what to do next when Rachel thought of the current history project. She copied in a simplified form enough panels for each child to do one; then carefully selecting suitable pieces from the ragbag the children built up the pictures in appliqué form. Finally the panels were joined and mounted and each child proudly signed his own work. They were extremely pleased with it, and it is the most effective piece of work they ever did.

Next came Knights and Castles, with which they had great fun. Mrs Hab knew all about castles, and they were soon immersed in pictures and models of castles, and talking knowledgeably about motte and bailey, bastions and inner fortifications. We had an elaborate model of a mediaeval castle complete with war machines and the right sort of soldiers; here were staged realistic battles which involved a great deal of argument about strategy and chronological exactitude - arguments which were settled in the bookroom. Heraldry proved a fascinating subject, and everyone designed his own coat of arms. Finally we went to the Tower of London and spent hours in the White Tower gazing at the armour and the weapons. We had been there before but this time there was new point added because the children understood something of the context of at least some of the things they were looking at. The thing that never failed to amuse them in the Tower was the difference in girth between the two suits of

Henry the Eighth's armour - one which fitted him as a young man, the other made for him in middle age.

It was the Tower and the suits of armour which got them interested in Henry the Eighth and his wives. We came home and read up the period, and then made a class book with pictures and family trees, stories and charts and diagrams. They really went to town on the Field of the Cloth of Gold, with lashings of gold paint and jewel colours like they had seen on some mediaeval manuscripts on one of our travels. They were also particularly taken with Mary, Queen of Scots; her tragic story was illustrated and dramatised and written up many times over. Needless to say they had a great time too with Queen Elizabeth the First, though they disapproved heartily of the shabby way she treated some of their heroes like Raleigh. Nevertheless she was fun to act, and even more fun to draw with her elaborate dresses.

Thus costume became their next passion; so, panting to keep up as they raced from topic to topic, I took them to the Victoria and Albert museum to see the real things. We also went to Windsor Castle; the girls were enchanted by the period dolls and the Queen's dolls' house, and the boys found a lot to interest them too. Deborah was fascinated by the furniture in the public rooms, and came home to construct period rooms, doll size, of her own. This was the time to fish out some painting books which I had put by for just such a moment; they were illustrated with the development of costume period by period and were very popular. So their interest in costume widened to take in furniture, then domestic architecture, transport and so on, and as far as they were concerned the development fell into five stages - mediaeval, Elizabethan, Regency, Victorian, and modern. We went to the Oxfordshire folk museum at Woodstock and saw the way kitchens looked in bygone days, and compared them with our mod. con. at home. (They also fastened each other in the old stocks which still stand outside the museum, just to get the feel of what it really felt like, they explained.) We went too to the Agricultural museum at Reading and marvelled at rural life in the not-so-distant past; here they recognised various familiar objects from the illustrations in the nursery rhyme book - the sort of spades that seem to go with 'digging and delving', the thatcher's tools propped against the wall when Jack was building his house, Little Bo Peep's crook, and so on. A year or two later we were able to go to York and see the Castle museum, which delighted them - it must surely be the best folk museum in the country, with its series of rooms furnished in the style of each period, both peasant and prosperous, and its street of nineteenth-century shops complete in every detail, including the tallow-makers and Terry's first sweet shop. The old streets and houses in York itself fascinated them too, with their gabled fronts and the overhanging upper storeys that practically meet in the middle.

In all this we never 'did history' as such. We never took notes or answered questions or checked what they had learned in any way. What they learned and what they remembered depended entirely on their own interest in the subject; perhaps in later years they will remember very little in detail, but I am sure that they will have a background knowledge which will help them to make sense of the details when they come to fill them in. Certainly when they were eight or nine and went to Madame Tussaud's, there was not much that they did not know something about, that did not connect up with one or other of their past projects.

On this particular visit it so happened that Madame Tussaud's had a special sort of 'Son et Lumière' programme on the Battle of Trafalgar. Now Nelson happened to be one of our heroes (we had many) so we paid our extra one-and-sixpence gladly and went in. We found ourselves on a life-sized replica of the *Victory* itself, with the battle of Trafalgar in full spate. The noise of the guns was deafening (though toned down for our comfort, we were assured, as the gunners themselves, many of them, were permanently deaf after the battle). We experienced the smoke and confusion of the lower deck where sweating stripped (wax) men toiled away at the guns, and in the cockpit were heart-broken to find Nelson himself dying - 'Oh why did he have to go up on deck like that - he was bound to be got by a sniper.'

'It was brave of him!'

'No, it was stupid. He should have taken off his medals at least so that no one would recognise him.'

'He was their leader, it was his duty - ' and so the argument raged. We were completely involved, and for the first time realised just how ghastly and terrifying those great sea battles must have been. The argument continued back in school, where we got out the books and followed the strategy, worked out Nelson's historic message to the fleet before the battle, and incidentally spent a happy week sending flag messages to each other and decoding them.

It once fell to my lot to teach geography to an 'O' level class, and I was amazed to discover how little they knew about the foods they ate and the clothes they wore. They had no idea, for instance, what a kipper was or how it had arrived on the fishmonger's slab; where silk and cotton came from; what paper was. It seemed to me that this sort of general knowledge was one thing we could usefully acquire at primary level at the same time as finding our way about the map of the world. The whole subject became known in our school as 'products' and for some months it featured quite largely in our activities.

With this in mind I had collected an assortment of visual aids, samples and charts and posters, from a variety of commercial firms. We had material on the production of coal, oil, paper, margarine, timber, milk and cheese, wool, chocolate, tea, coffee, cotton, rubber, and almost any other commodity you can think of. I had also acquired a life-size model of a cocoa-pod and a box of samples showing the production stages of chocolate; more samples showing the production stages of wool, cotton, silk, and paper; and a box of samples of raw minerals. Once the subject had been studied, these samples were left in the room so that the children could go back to them at any time, handle them as much as they needed to until they could really understand.

Our interest in wool, emanating from stories about Australia, began with collecting our own wool from the hedgerows, cleaning it, and dyeing it with home-made vegetable dyes. Next we tried carding, spinning, and weaving it; testing it for shrinkage and colour-fastness; knitting; and finally an expedition in the spring to watch the sheep being sheared. I tried to take them to a nearby blanket factory, but the reply to my request, as at the local paper mill and the Bourneville chocolate factory, was that they were too young - which of course was nonsense.

Sometimes we tackled the products by way of the country, as with India. We read books about life in India, found it on the map, talked about the climate. We wore caste-marks and saris for a day and played at being an Indian family, with all the props carefully worked out from the books. We made a card model of an Indian village, talked about the animals - read lots of Kipling - and about the clothes and the food, then about the crops, and so worked round to tea and rice, cotton and silk. I thought of getting silkworms for the children to look after until I read that they had to be kept in the airing cupboard and fed at frequent intervals through the night; I felt that after four children I had done my share of that sort of thing, and gave my mind to a visit to Lullingstone silk farm instead. The tea trade in the Far East put me in mind of the *Cutty Sark*, the old tea clipper moored at Greenwich; here we saw how they used to pack the hold and even the sides of the ship with bales of English wool going out, and replaced them with tea-chests of the same size and shape coming back. The collection of old figure-heads in the hold fascinated the children, as well as the rigging of the old sailing ship, and they came back to school with a new passion - ships.

We chugged happily down the Thames drinking in every detail of the docks as we passed, and spent hours hanging over the wharf in the Pool of London watching timber and bananas being unloaded. I found a model of a sailing-ship that one of my sons had made - we borrowed it and kept it on the windowsill. We drew boats, read about them, and traced their development from a dug-out canoe to the *Queen Mary*. We became experts on rigging and talked knowledgeably about schooners and ketches. We read all the 'Tommy the Tugboat' books, and a little series about tugs and barges and river traffic generally. We took a steamer down the river just for the fun of going through the numerous locks; on one of our walks we stopped and gave the lock-keeper a hand for an hour or so in order to understand just how the thing really works.

The climax of our joy was due to a strike which crippled Southampton docks. We guessed, rightly, that because of the strike more ships than usual would be berthed there. To our delight we found not only the *Queen Mary*, but several of the big Castle Line ships - the docks were jammed with liners and cargo boats of all shapes and sizes. We hired a little boat and went chugging in and out among the giants, right under the hull of the *Queen Mary*, so close that we were all able to touch its towering black sides - the sheer size of the thing from that angle was overwhelming. We heard how before the Captain could even see Southampton, and was still twelve miles out he had to reverse the engines in order to stop the great ship before it went crashing through the town itself - quite a thought, that. We gazed wonderingly at ships of all sizes, some with mysterious names printed in strange hieroglyphics on their sides, and speculated on where they came from and what they were carrying. Some tugs were berthing a ship that had just arrived - apparently they were not on strike - and by a stroke of luck found a banana boat from the West Indies being unloaded, perhaps because of its perishable cargo.

When we had seen everything and I was just rounding up everybody to go home, there was an objection from Sebbie:

'We can't go yet - we haven't seen any oil-tankers.' I gazed hopelessly down Southampton Water where the oil refineries were just visible in the distance - there simply wasn't time to go there that day, so the objection had to be over-ruled.

In school the next day I produced a Meccano model dockyard that my own boys had played with, and for weeks this was arranged and rearranged - one gathered that there was no strike on here.

It was another of the Ladybird books that introduced the subject of coalmining, and then oil, gas, and power generally. I knew there was no hope of taking such young children down a coalmine or even round the local gasworks, but we did the next best thing and spent a happy day in the children's gallery at the London Science museum. Here we went through the mock-up of a coalmine (not a very modern one, but it gave us the feel), and saw working models illustrating the development of power from animal-worked wells to electricity.

We paid several visits to the Science museum and the children always found something new to intrigue them there. On another occasion the theme was 'transport', when the exhibition in the Children's Gallery took us exhaustively from the first log-rollers to jet airliners. Edward had been talking for weeks about Stevenson's *Rocket* and couldn't wait to see it in the flesh, so to speak. He led us feverishly all round the ground floor in search of it and then suddenly there it was, the real thing. We gazed reverently - for once even Edward was quite speechless with emotion. Graham was more interested in modern speed and shot off to the top floor in search of the aircraft; here I found him blissfully seated in the cockpit of a Second-war fighter - it always rather shakes me that these children regard the Spitfire as a museum piece. We also had a glorious time climbing in and out of old Sheffield trams (these children had never seen a working tram) and early locomotives. They loved, as I do, the beautiful shining brass and polished levers of the steam engines; I wished they could have known the thrill of these mighty dragons roaring through a station at full speed - the diesel engine is a poor substitute. The museum guards were a bit mean at the Science museum and did not really like the children touching their treasures, though how you can be expected to understand something that you are not allowed to feel I don't know. We were made much more welcome at the Transport museum in York, where the kindly Yorkshiremen welcomed the children's interest and lifted them up into the driver's cab so that they could pretend to drive the engines for themselves.

Next door to the Science museum is the Geological museum; one day we popped in here to see what precious stones look like in the raw and see pictures of how they are mined. This gave us much food for thought; as soon as we got home we rushed to our own mineral collection to see if we had anything worth selling. Apparently we hadn't, but that did not stop us keeping a hopeful eye open for likely-looking bits of rock whenever we were out in the country. After all, we knew now what to look for, and you never know -

One of our favourite haunts and sources of information was the Commonwealth Institute in London: we made several trips here when the children were aged between six and eight or nine and learned a tremendous lot. Though it only deals with Commonwealth countries, between them they cover most of the world's products, and everything is so well displayed that no one could fail to understand and remember. To give one or two examples; in the section on West Africa there is a model of a cocoa plantation with real life-size trees hung with golden pods. Wax figures with knives are hacking open some pods and putting the seeds to dry in the sun. Nearby more figures were using hand hoes and growing (in real earth) yams and sweet potatoes. Elsewhere we saw groundnuts growing against glass, and realised why they are so called. There were detailed dioramas of sugar and coffee plantations, tea gardens, cotton farms. The natural fauna and flora of countries as far apart as India and Canada were clearly and attractively displayed.

It would have been impossible to take in everything in one visit, so each time we went we had some specific subject in mind. Once it was a study of farming in West Africa. The children had paper to write notes and draw what they saw, but we did not make detailed notebooks when we got back to the classroom; we just discussed what we had seen, sometimes drew pictures or made models, and it gave new colour to stories about Nigeria or Ghana.

Another time the brief was to find out about certain products, how they were grown and processed, and where. On yet another occasion I gave them each a list of questions to which they had to discover the answers by searching all over the Institute. This took the form of a competition, and the next day there were prizes for the best efforts in each of two age-groups.

We always visited the Institute's shop before we left and bought treasures for the schoolroom - silk flags of the Commonwealth countries, colour postcards of the dioramas, cardboard models to make of villages in Fiji, India, or Ceylon; and books for the class library.

The Mediterranean countries were of particular interest to these children because several of them had been there for summer holidays - Jose, Catherine and Elwyn to Greece, Graham to Italy, Nicky and Sebbie to France. Jose brought back a collection of fruits she had found growing in Greece, including a prickly pear, which gave some trouble - it was more deadly than gorse. She made a display of them in the bookroom, after replacing the citrus fruits and olives, grapes and figs which had died on the way home.

Whenever I saw exotic and unusual fruits in the market I bought some for the children to try. Most of them, we decided, must be an acquired taste, but Nicky would always finish everyone else's share with a happy smile - I don't think that we ever found one that he did not like.

America too was a country that held great interest for us, particularly as so many of the children's nursery companions had been American and we still heard from some of them. Pioneer stories had always been popular, and we had a beautiful model of a covered wagon, complete in every detail, which inspired many games. Davy Crockett and Wyatt Earp were nursery heroes, and Red Indians took their colour from Hiawatha and Tiger Lily. We had a jigsaw puzzle of the states of America - Graham could do it in four minutes flat without reference to the picture, but then he had been to America and was our resident expert on the subject. Nicky had also been (they both had fathers whose work had taken them across the Atlantic), but his chief memory was of the Natural History museum in New York where he had seen the skeleton of a real dinosaur - the biggest in the world, he assured us. This had inspired in him a passionate interest in prehistoric animals - in fact he developed a positive fixation about dinosaurs; he drew them, talked about them, played at being one, until we were all desperately trying to divert him to some new passion. When the interest in prehistoric animals was at its height - we had quite a presentable dinosaur slung impressively from the roof in our own museum, which we had been to see - I had brought out a rather gruesome collection of plastic models and labelled them to the best of my ability as brontosaurus, pterodactyl, etc., but I was not allowed to get away with such scientific inexactitude. Nicky, whom I would have sworn was hardly reading yet, removed two of my labels firmly and politely suggested that I should look them up in a book because he was sure that I had got them wrong. I did so, and I had, though just to keep my end up I pleaded that the models were so bad that one could not be sure what they were supposed to be.

To sidetrack a little, these animal fixations of small children have always interested me. Sebbie had a similar obsession with lobsters, though this was partly because the word itself amused him, but for months he drew endless pictures of lobsters, talked about them, wrote stories about them. With Antonia it was cats - never any other animal that I remember - which inspired her first stories, poems, pictures. One of my own sons insisted for some years that he was a rhinoceros; I don't remember that he drew them or wrote stories about them - he just was one. It seems an odd choice, not even a very attractive creature, but perhaps it was something to do with a rhino's ability to ride roughshod through life unafraid of man or beast and totally unthwarted - an enviable position, I imagine, from a small boy's viewpoint.

All these trips were backed up by work in the classroom - wider reading, model-making, pictures, writing. One of our projects concerned 'famous people'; we were great hero-worshippers and each had our own favourites. On this occasion the children were left to do their own research and choose their own subject, and then to mount an exhibition to commend their particular hero or heroine to the rest of the class. A prize was offered for the best effort, and their parents were to come and see their work. There was much secret preparation in the bookroom, the workroom, and at home, and the final result was an interesting series of tables devoted to such diverse characters as Marco Polo, Nelson, David Livingstone, Grace Darling, and so on. The winning entry was Catherine's on Florence Nightingale; she had made a nicely detailed model of a field hospital in the Crimean war, complete with the Lady with the Lamp, and had also written and illustrated a book about her.

When Elwyn and Edward and Antonia joined us we tried to think up some trips more geared to their age and interests. One sure winner was the zoo: all the children were interested in animals. We had already been to Whipsnade, so this time we went to Regent's Park - led by an enthusiastic Nicky anxious to show us the new Nocturnal Mammal house and the Snowden Aviary. That was a very successful trip, and included rides on ponies and elephants and in a llama cart. It was on this occasion that we watched chickens hatching in an incubator:

'I never knew it took so long,' said Rebecca. 'It doesn't tell you that in books. In stories there's a knocking from inside the shell, it cracks, and pop! there's the chicken. It's not at all like that really, is it?'

We also watched chimpanzees being trained to get bananas out of a locked cupboard, and this sparked off a discussion about the intelligence of various animals. After some argument several children were seen rushing off to the Children's Zoo armed with bags of peanuts to put their theories to the test.

One day we went to the local fire station; the firemen were very kind and let the children climb up into the fire-engine, try on the helmets, and ring the bell. One of the men demonstrated how to slide down the pole - this amused the children so much that they were all for having one in school to save walking down the stairs at playtime. Then they ran out one of the engines and raised the extension ladder to show how it worked - though to the children's chagrin I refused to let them climb up too.

Another time we went to the Sorting Office and saw what happened to our letters and parcels before they reached us. The postmen were grilled about how they prevented mail robberies, which of the big hampers of parcels were destined for our particular parts of the town, and what they did with the letters without any stamps on them - this last was an anxious inquiry with personal significance. We watched a machine franking letters too fast for us to count, and we marvelled at the speed and accuracy of the sorters.

We went to all sorts of places just round and about - sometimes only with the older children if we thought the younger ones would be bored. We went to the county agricultural show, to fairs and local museums, to gymkhanas on village greens, to a mannequin parade. Once we watched a man blowing glass animals; another time we went to see a prehistoric fort. We flew kites on the Downs, and explored little Cotswold towns with their broad streets and their lovely mellow stone houses. We wandered through quiet water-meadows and saw a kingfisher dive into the stream, and herons fishing in the shallows. Once or twice we went to Bourton-on-the-Water and visited the model village (a never-failing fascination this), and to the special Bird zoo there; here we saw king-penguins diving for fish, and in the tropical birdhouse watched humming-birds hovering to feed from the tubes hung from the trees.

Of all our excursions I think perhaps our regular 'nature walks' were the ones I liked best. Every spring we would set off in wellingtons, armed with jam jars on string, and fishing nets tied on to long bamboo canes, and make for a shallow stream we knew of nearby. With luck we would be early enough to find the spawn before it hatched so that we could watch the whole process, and one year we found both frog- and toad-spawn so that we could compare the two. We became experts in pond fauna and flora and our aquaria were never empty; sometimes we had a whole collection of bowls and dishes housing different kinds of pond life - their care was a complicated and time-consuming business. After the frogs hatched we fed them lovingly for as long as we could on greenfly specially cultivated on the roses that grew over the yard-wall; when finally we had to let them go we turned them loose on the nearest pond - which happened to be in the University Botanical Gardens; I hope they like frogs - we must have been responsible for quite a colony of them there.

On one occasion we had gone tiddler-fishing in the local park, but were having a bad day. We had drawn the shallows for nearly an hour, getting very wet in the process, but without a single catch. We had decided to call it a day and were wandering home along the bank of the river when somebody spotted a shoal of tiny fish, so we thought we would have one more dip. There was tremendous excitement when the net came up with several wriggling silver bodies in it, but someone had already emptied the water out of the jam jar and Sebbie all but took a header into the river in his hurry to refill it. I was flat in the mud helping to land the catch safely, and we were all so intent on the operation that we were unaware of somebody bending over us and addressing me in incredulous tones:

'Good Heavens! My dear, it *is* you. What on earth are you doing?' It was an elderly friend, a headmistress in whose school I had once taught, and whose view of the dignity of the teaching profession did not include lying in the mud fishing for tiddlers. However the tiddlers were a great success and lived in our tank for nearly six months, after which we turned them loose again.

Sometimes we went to watch and feed the deer at another park in the town - on one occasion to settle an argument about what sort they were; we had just been reading that there are three different types of deer in Britain. Sometimes we went to the tropical houses at the Botanical Gardens and looked at the giant cacti - we wondered whether our own miniature specimens would ever grow as big as that if only we fed them right, but thought again that perhaps they were more convenient as they were. We saw real banana plants there and understood how enormous the leaves really are. We watched tropical fish swimming about in the warm water, and the lush vegetation growing so densely all round, gasped for breath in the hot humid air and understood what a tropical rain forest feels like.

Each year we went to see the swans and ducks and moorhens nesting by the river, and watched with excitement to count each season's new brood as they hatched. We fed them on the cold winter days, and one day, tossing bread to the mallards on the pond in the park, noticed that we were also feeding a colony of rats who had nested under the bank among the thick reeds. We watched them for half an hour as they darted out furtively to snatch the bread and shuffle home with it to their holes - they too had to eat. Early in the spring we went to see the new lambs, and to search for the spring bulbs as they appeared in due order, snowdrops, aconites, crocuses, scillas. We always planted our own bulbs too in the boxes in the yard as well as indoors, but the ones we found growing wild were more precious, a surer promise of spring.

Sometimes we just walked and looked and watched without any particular aim in view. We would stop on the bridge to play pooh-sticks, or lie in the deep grass and watch the miniature world that lives at ground level; lift up big stones to see what was underneath, taking care to put them back afterwards as we found them; watch a kestrel hovering high up in the sky before it dropped like a stone on some hapless prey; listen to skylarks or grasshoppers or the harsh cries of a pair of jays as they flapped through the tall trees above us; watch the rooks rebuilding their nests in the same old trees where we had watched them the year before, or wasps buzzing in and out of their nest in the spindle tree. These walks were always so peaceful; usually as we wandered along chattering happily I would have a child on either hand - and not always the youngest. Now and then one or two children would dart off to investigate something that had caught their eye; sometimes we all fell silent, just watching and thinking. There was rarely any argument or acrimony on these occasions.

Summer and winter we went swimming. In winter, once everybody had outgrown the Tadpole club (the little teaching pool) and could at least keep afloat, we went to the indoor full-size pool once or twice a week. Sometimes we managed to fix up some professional coaching for the older ones in crawl and diving, and Jose at least developed later into a good swimmer. The boys by this time had joined us, but they never enjoyed it as much as the girls. As a rule several of the parents joined the children in the water, which made it much more fun for the children.

In the summer we went every Thursday after morning school to an open-air pool in the next town, taking a picnic lunch with us. There we would be joined by as many of the parents and brothers and sisters as could get away, and spent a blissful afternoon in the water and sunbathing on the green lawns which stretched beside the river. When we had swum and sunned ourselves into a state of exhaustion we would repair to the park over the way, which boasted one of the best collections of slides, swings, and seesaws in the district, according to the connoisseurs.

The children always found water irresistible. One summer day I took them to a park on the edge of the town where they had not been before and where there was a small collection of animals and birds that I thought might interest them, including a white peacock who might be persuaded to show his paces for them. The children wanted to run ahead and explore so they whooped off into the distance while I followed more slowly. As I rounded the corner my gaze fell on the children, stark naked, disporting themselves joyfully in the paddling pool, to the utter consternation of a handful of highly respectable matrons who were seated round the pool overseeing their own well-covered offspring; these worthy citizens were muttering about it being 'disgusting' and 'not very nice', though myself I thought they looked charming, and as there was no one else around I could not think what harm they were doing. To the children water was simply enjoyable stuff that you play with, but you don't want to get your clothes wet so you take them off first. I could not think of any sensible reason to give them for asking them to get dressed again:

'These people (mothers all, with small children of their own) don't like to see you without your clothes on.'

'Why not?'

'It just isn't done.'

'What do you mean? Why isn't it done?' - and so on.

In the end I simply urged them to hurry up and come and see the peacock, and quite happily they threw their clothes back on and rushed off in a new direction. Of course the problem solved itself as they grew older and developed a natural modesty, though they never had any false modesty amongst themselves.

In this chapter I have tried to show how the children learned through their own experience, by following up their interests in whatever way was open to them, exploring the subject through reading, seeing the real thing, trying it out for themselves; understanding what they had seen and done by talking about it, writing about it, painting or drawing it or reproducing it in model form, until they had fully absorbed the experience and made it their own. To do all this they needed the mechanical skills of language, writing, and maths, and these were not neglected, but such skills were only ever a means to an end, never an end in themselves.

If we had had a school motto - but we didn't, we were not that sort of school - it might have been (with apologies to Caesar) 'veni, vidi, feci'.

CHAPTER 6

Work and Play

While the older children explored the new world of books, the little ones learned to read. Surrounded as they were by the spoils of literacy they were tremendously eager to follow their elders, and though they followed the same paths they covered the ground much more quickly. They caught the passion for story writing and produced vivid narratives - sometimes difficult to follow because of a pre-Johnsonian fluidity of spelling, but full of original turns of phrase and imaginative description. Once we had a book competition; each child, even Elwyn who was then aged four, wrote and illustrated an original story in the form of a home-made book, and someone was brought in from outside to award two prizes for the two different age groups. I would like to have kept their efforts - they were amusing, refreshing, alive, charmingly illustrated - but their proud authors were anxious to take them home.

The little ones, always with the example of the older children's work to inspire them, were soon making picture books of insects, transport, birds, or anything else that interested them. They would search in the bookroom for relevant pictures and then plague anyone who happened to be around to decipher the more difficult words for them so that they could extract the information they wanted.

Every day alongside the creative writing we spent a certain amount of time learning routine skills. The younger ones did phonetic drill - word-building and reading through the wall-charts where the words were grouped phonetically - and also learned to spell a short list of words from their reading-book. Various mothers still came in daily to hear them read individually. The older children worked their way through a pile of fifty 'spelling cards' on which I had grouped all the words which came within a child's common writing vocabulary, but whose spelling did not conform to the phonetic rules. There was a certain competitiveness to get through all these routine tasks faster than one's neighbour, and the industrious were rewarded with 'stars'.

Everybody worked through the same series of workbooks. At first these were designed to give extra reading and writing practice, and then to help with phonetic word-building. By the time the child was reading fluently the workbooks were designed to cope painlessly with grammar, comprehension, sentence-construction, and all the related subjects usually grouped under the heading of English Language. Each child worked his way through these at his own pace; I was there to help when necessary, and I checked the books from time to time. Mistakes had to be corrected, and no one could proceed to a new workbook until he had completed the previous one properly. Sometimes I would give a specific lesson on one of the points dealt with in the workbooks - for example 'nouns, verbs, and adjectives' - but for the most part the workbooks were self-explanatory. There was no restriction of time spent on them; the children could take them out and get on with them whenever they had nothing else specifically to do.

For the first hour of each morning each child would have a certain number of tasks to do. He would take his turn at reading individually; he would also learn his quota of spellings for the day and have them checked. In addition he would be given a specific task - perhaps a 'work card' to do, or a story to read with questions to answer on it, or a particular subject to 'find out' about. Once he had done these things he was free to get on with his workbook, or to get on with a private or class project, or to write a story, read a book, draw a picture, or learn a poem. When the little ones tired they played with toys or Plasticine or paint, but the bigger ones seemed by this time to be bored with such nursery occupations. As long as a child was busy and interested he was allowed to get on undisturbed, and apart from necessary routine learning, to choose what he would do.

The 'work cards' consisted of an informative text, accompanied by an attractive illustration, on one side, and on the other, questions to test comprehension, suggestions for practical work - drawing, modelling, etc. - and more suggestions for further reading; I had already arranged that the books suggested were available in the bookroom. We had over a hundred of these cards, and the child was allowed to choose which one he wanted to do; if on a certain day none of them appealed, then I suggested that he thought up something different that he would like to do - it always seems to me a complete waste of time to make someone read or write about something that does not interest him. The result was that the children were never bored - there was always something that completely absorbed their interest, and they were given a lot of time to follow their own particular line of inquiry.

They were free too to move around the room as they wished, or to leave it without permission. They rarely abused this freedom, and when occasionally I realised that perhaps a couple of them had been missing for some time, it was often simply that they had met in the bookroom and got deeply absorbed in conversation.

Some days we devoted the minimum time to routine tasks in order to get on with a new project. This always began with a general discussion to decide on scope and presentation and to allot jobs (even the smallest participated in some way), then everyone would rush off to do his bit with enthusiasm; I should add that I too was allotted my share of the work. Those who could read would be detailed off to look up different angles of the subject; those who could not would look for suitable pictures in the scrap-box, or tear up paper ready for the papier mâché, or paint the sky on the back-drop for a model. The practical work was done in small groups, a little child in each group so that the older ones could explain what was going on and how they could help. For the most part the older children were surprisingly patient and gentle with the little ones, and were rewarded with the uncritical admiration and devotion of which only small children are capable.

I have already mentioned the need to encourage children to read full-length books for themselves. When they have just learned to read there is a tendency for them to want to read only very easy stories; there are usually plenty of these about, and sometimes they just stick at this stage, happy to read comics but never making the final effort needed for sustained reading. Obviously there are a great many children who never do reach the stage of reading for pleasure - witness the number of adults who will only ever read picture papers. Therefore they need as much help and encouragement to overcome this hurdle as they do at the beginning. Once our children had learned to read they then progressed to simple readers - we had dozens of these, with clear print and attractive pictures, and they could be read from cover to cover in fifteen minutes at the most.[1] Then came more

[1] It is possible to get lists of these readers from their publishers, but they

advanced readers with a collection of rather longer stories - here the child was handling a full-length book, and if he felt inclined he could go on from one story to the next. By this time he was used to reading from a 'proper' book, and it was but a short step to tackling the same sort of book with a full-length story. It was at this stage that we found the Puffin paperbacks invaluable, though anyone under six tended to find the print rather close.

Every day I read them at least one story, often introducing them to books which they would then go and read for themselves. 'Milly-Molly-Mandy' was always very popular with the younger ones; they were so intrigued by the map of the village in the front of the book that we invented a village of our own called Picklebury. We drew a map of it, then made a model of it; we decided who lived in each house and then wrote stories about the people we had invented.

Other stories beloved of the small children were about 'Little Pete' and 'My Naughty Little Sister' - the latter provoked much discussion, and everybody's sympathies were with the little sister; we concluded that the poor child had a very stupid family.

Everybody liked fairy stories, including some of the traditional English ones all about 'Laidly Worms' and other such fascinating creatures; these provoked a spate of original monsters, both painted and modelled, which apparently enjoyed adventures more weird and exciting than anything suggested by tradition. Rosemary Manning's dragon in 'Green Smoke' was another favourite.

Besides the good solid traditional folk tales there was a whole field of delightful whimsy by Stella Mead and

---

are difficult to obtain in bookshops. Try putting pressure on your local bookseller.

Alison Uttley. The sheer magic of Peter Pan never wore off, but even more beloved was the American 'Wizard of Oz', though this was partly due to the beautiful pictures in the edition we had.

Then there was the fun of Mrs Pepperpot, and Pooh, Mary Poppins, and Professor Branestawm; the Heath Robinson illustrations in the latter set all the children off inventing and drawing complicated machines of their own which gave rise to much merriment as well as some understanding of how levers, pulleys, cogs and springs work. We also made up our own Pooh hums, and invented new scrapes for Mrs Pepperpot. When they were a bit older Dr Dolittle was very popular; and in a different way they enjoyed Kipling as long as it was read to them - they found the 'Just So' stories too difficult to read for themselves. When they were six or seven 'Alice' and the Arthurian legends gave them more to bite on, and Tove Jansson's 'Moomintroll' books provided charming light relief.

Familiarity with the nursery rhymes in the early days grew into a love of words for their own sake, and I read them a great deal of poetry. To begin with I picked out short easy poems that I knew they would understand, and after reading them aloud I wrote each one out in script on a card and drew a little picture to go with it. These cards were kept in a box on the shelf, and if a child had taken a fancy to a particular one he could take the card out and learn it, or copy it into his own private anthology - most of them had made books for this purpose, and here they recorded their own favourites in their best writing, often charmingly illustrated. They soon began to search both at home and in the bookroom for new treasures, and if the others liked what they had found these too were added to the card collection.

Deborah once came across

You spotted snakes with double tongue,
Thorny hedgehogs, be not seen;

etc., from 'Midsummer Night's Dream', and was so entranced with it that I told them the story of Oberon and Titania's quarrel, and picked out some more of the delightful verses for them to learn. We listened to Mendelssohn's music to the play, and it provided us with material for mime and dance and painting. I told them too a condensed version of 'The Tempest', and Ariel's songs were added to our collection.

Extracts from Hiawatha gave them great pleasure too - such wonderful words to roll round the tongue, and colourful scenes to paint. R. L. Stevenson's *Garden of Verses* appealed to some of the younger children, along with some of the lesser known traditional rhymes that we dug up out of our exhaustive book on the subject - things like

There was an old woman lived under a hill
And if she's not gone she lives there still;
Baked apples she sold, and cranberry pies,
And she's the old woman who never told lies!

and

Three young rats in black felt hats,
Three young ducks in white straw flats,
Three young dogs with curling tails,
Three young cats with demi-veils,
Went out to walk with two young pigs
In satin vests and sorrel wigs.
But suddenly it chanced to rain,
And so they all ran home again.

There was another nice one about King Arthur making a 'bag-pudding' with some stolen barley-meal; he is described as 'stuffing it well with plums', and adding 'great lumps of fat as big as my two thumbs', suet pudding with a vengeance - it seems that even the iron-stomached courtiers of those days were unable to finish it, because we are told that 'what they could not eat that night, the Queen next morning fried'.

On a higher plane Christina Rossetti's 'Goblin Market' was another favourite. At one time we had a great passion for Lewis Carroll, Lear, Hilaire Belloc, and de la Mare. The children would chant the chorus with relish as I read 'Calico Pie' or 'the Jumblies', write their own limericks after Lear, and savour bits of the 'Hunting of the Snark' in retrospect with delighted chuckles. Later they loved T. S. Eliot's 'Old Possum's Book of Practical Cats'. When we were reading the Arthurian legends the 'Lady of Shalott' appealed to their imagination as it had done to mine.

Always after hearing a story or a poem they were given a large sheet of paper and time to draw a picture if they wanted to. It was these sessions that produced their most vivid pictures as they grew older - though the pictures with most movement, that is with the really living three-dimensional figures - grew out of their own experience in the music-and-movement classes.

A few minutes every day were spent on writing practice, even after the children had developed a cursive hand. Each person had a book from which he could copy individual letters or passages in italic script - based on oval letters rather than round ones - and most of them were in the end capable of a clear and elegant hand. Unfortunately several of them later went to schools where a far-from-elegant hand, with bun-shaped letters and a proliferation of loops, was in vogue, and they were made to conform, with the result that their own individual style was lost. The fact that they were capable of an elegant hand did not of course mean that their every-day writing was always good; they were usually in such a tearing hurry to get words on to paper, their thoughts racing ahead of their hands, that their writing degenerated into an illegible scrawl; but the basic motor habits were there and in time did influence the formation of a mature hand.

The other basic discipline to which we allotted a great deal of time was maths. I have described how in the nursery years we established a firm understanding of the numbers up to ten, learned to count up to a hundred, and to write and recognise the numbers. After that came 'tens and units', which were explained by bundles of ten sticks done up in an elastic band, or by packets of ten sweets (though I had to abandon this method when all the sweets were eaten one playtime - the temptation was suddenly too much for certain sweet-toothed members, as I ought to have foreseen!). There had also been a great deal of practice in weighing things; drawing lines with rulers; pouring water, rice, sand, beans, or anything else fluid enough from one container into another; shop-play handling real pennies, sixpences, and threepenny bits; measuring things in terms of so many hands, or lengths of string, or so-and-so's feet; but all this without reference to formal arithmetic.

At this stage I introduced various parallel activities, the first of which was the Cuisenaire rods. These are lengths of wood in units of one centimetre, two centimetres, and so on up to ten centimetres, with a specific colour for each length - thus the one-centimetre rod is white, the two-centimetre rod is red, and so on. The fact that they are measured in centimetres and not in inches is irrelevant because what matters is their length relative to one another. To begin with the children simply play with them, build pyramids with them, and discover for themselves the relationship of one to another. For instance they soon realise that two red rods and a wh te rod are the same length as a yellow rod. They then write down simple equations to represent their discoveries, but calling the rods by their colours - they have not yet attached numbers to them. So the discovery cited above would be written $2r+w=y$. Then they discover that a pink rod and a white one are also the same length as a yellow one, so they can now write $p+w=y$, and then $2r+w=p+w$, and therefore $2r=p$.

Subtraction is demonstrable by covering up one rod with another. You take for instance a yellow rod and you take away from it a pink rod (that is, you place the pink rod on top of the yellow rod and observe how much of the yellow rod is left showing, what rod would fit into the space that is left). And you write it as $y-p=w$, or as $p+w=y$, or as $y-w=p$.

Multiplication and division are equally practicable; if you want to cover an orange (ten centimetre) rod with red ones you discover that you need five of them; so $o=5r$ or $o=5\times r$. Or you can put the red rods underneath the orange one and write what you see $\frac{o}{r}=5$. You then learn that because of this the red rod is said to be one fifth of the orange rod - an idea quite easy to grasp after you have discovered it for yourself in concrete terms like this. And so you come to take fractions, even sixteenth or twenty-thirds, as a straightforward way of describing demonstrable facts. In fact I found that five and six-year-olds coped quite happily with simple algebraic equations and fractions in this way.

This algebraic approach to number gives the children considerable facility in both handling and recording quantity and of understanding numbers in concrete terms, though after a few months they dispense with the rods except when they are trying to master a new process. On the other hand I did not want to rely entirely on the Cuisenaire system, and so it was only one of several approaches.

We also tackled number from the arithmetical angle. We had various picture books which I used with half a dozen children at a time; we discussed the pictures and made up stories about them which involved counting the objects, adding, subtracting, multiplying and dividing them. We had other similar very attractive picture books with which the children worked on their own - here they had to work out a sum in their heads and write the answer on a 'ticket' (a small square of paper) which they then placed on the paper until I came round to check what they had done. This obviated the need for a lot of tedious writing and setting out in books, and gave priority instead to the mathematical problem involved. This was the principal on which we always worked - what mattered was the maths, not the writing out - and it meant that far more time was devoted to real number work and the children did not get bored (at this age they find writing a considerable strain); they also learned to work everything out as far as possible in their heads.

In teaching early maths I have always avoided teaching 'rules'. The child must understand exactly what he is doing in concrete terms - if from his own discoveries he comes to evolve his own rules, that is an entirely different matter. If however he can only solve a problem by remembering the 'rule', he is utterly helpless the minute he forgets the rule if he does not really understand what he is doing.

From the beginning I left them to solve every problem in whatever way seemed best to them - often we compared the various ways in which different people had arrived at the answer. Also I encouraged them to do as much as possible of the working in their heads - we never bothered with neat rows of figures; the important things were the reasoning out of the problem and the answer. It was only when they were due to go to other schools that I taught them to set sums out neatly and show all the working - I could imagine how their usual hieroglyphic jottings would be received at a formal school! The fact remained that they knew what they were doing and did not often get the answer wrong.

As in English we had a series of arithmetic workbooks through which each child worked at his own pace. These simply dealt with the arithmetical processes, but gave ample practice so that by the time the child had worked through them he was absolutely sure of all his tables and of all the number bonds up to ten, which in turn meant that he could cope with all bonds because he also understood the principle of place-value.

Alongside these 'practice books' we also did a great deal of practical work. For one thing we had a lot of games, both home-made and bought. For instance there was a card game on the lines of 'snap' in which the object was to recognise the bonds of ten; there were various board games which involved rapid addition and subtraction; one very popular board game which involved saving and changing money and buying toys with it. Another involved delivering milk to houses and reckoning in pints, quarts, and gallons, measurements with which we were already familiar through games at the sink. We played 'Put and Take' with all the avidity of seasoned gamblers, and we fished for paper fish with numbers on the back which we totted up with lightning speed to find the biggest catch.

We arranged counters and animals and little wooden men in rows and patterns until all the lower tables were absorbed by experience. Later I introduced the subject of factors through the Cuisenaire colours, and seven-year-olds played complicated games with cards and charts on which numbers were represented by symbols coloured according to their factors. This game, which they enjoyed playing, finally consolidated their grasp of the multiplication tables, most of which they had absorbed without rote learning.

We had a game on the 'Fizz-buzz' theme where the object was to recognise prime numbers - you count rapidly round the group substituting the word 'prime' for every number without factors (prime, prime, prime, four, prime, six, prime, eight, nine, ten, prime, and so on), and if you make a mistake you are out.

'Sets' were regarded as great fun by the five-year-olds. First of all we laid coloured plastic hoops on the floor and built up sets from a box of assorted toys, leaves, conkers and so on; then we would draw what we had made. Later the children drew their own hoops and drew the objects inside them. This play established the idea of what sets are, and from this foundation it was an easy step to the proper use of sets and Venn diagrams.

'Area' was understood by grids of transparent plastic laid over pieces of coloured card - you simply counted the squares (this of course after much experience of covering space in various ways at the play stage - laying a table-cloth, covering a book with tiles, or the table with many small hands). Counting the squares over a triangle presented difficulties until it occured to someone to put two triangles together to make a rectangle - which proved a much simpler proposition. On such occasions I resisted the temptation to point out the short cut - it would have been valueless if the child had not discovered it for himself.

To demonstrate fractions we cut up Plasticine cakes, folded paper, drew shapes and coloured them in sections, divided sweets among the group - as well as the work we did with the rods. As with everything else it was not a case of explaining the thing once and everyone understanding for ever after, but a gradual build-up of experience of the same law in dozens of different ways, a steady absorption of the way things behave over a long period of time, so that in the end you come to know what 'a quarter' or 'a tenth' means in the same way as you know what cold water feels like, or what someone means when he says he has seen a dog, even though there isn't one in the room.

Plane geometry grew from a great deal of work with shapes - shapes discovered in the environment, through pattern-making with coloured sticky paper; solid geometry derived from model-making with tins and blocks and boxes, and took in work on volume on the way.

As well as the 'practice' workbooks each child worked through a series of three workbooks by Mollie Clarke which I thought were particularly useful and attractive - 'I Can Measure', 'I Can Weigh', and 'I Can Use Coins'. They had lots of pictures which could be coloured and set lots of practical problems on the lines of: 'Weigh an ounce of flour and an ounce of peas and put them into separate jars; which takes up more room?' They provided enjoyable practical experience of weighing, measuring, and money, and again the child could get on at his own pace without having to wait for others to keep up with him.

We had a marvellous piece of furniture that I had had specially made which was known as 'the maths corner'. It consisted of an L-shaped counter with roomy storage shelves below to house our 'maths equipment' - scales and weights, cannisters and baskets of various things to weigh; boxes of tape-measures, rulers, balls of string, endless rolls of coloured paper streamers; cubes for calculating volume, grids for measuring area; cardboard coins and real money; jars, boxes, containers of all sorts; geometrical solids, cardboard geometrical shapes; counters of every shape and size; and nail-boards, which were simply boards with nails hammered into them at various intervals and in varying geometrical patterns, and the idea was to stretch elastic bands over these to make triangles, rectangles, and so on - they were endlessly useful in elementary geometry.

This counter was the centre for practical maths, and anyone could go there to work whenever he needed to.

The daily maths session was divided into half written work and half practical. During the written work everyone kept quiet - it was one of the few periods when talking was banned, on the grounds that no one could think properly if someone else was chattering. I went through each child's work every day and the practice book immediately illuminated any point that the child had not grasped. Then I could go over the difficulty with him individually and if necessary prescribe remedial practical work to help him understand. This system meant that every child acquired a solid grounding with no gaps - if he was away ill he was simply that much behind in his own programme. Moreover because everyone had work to get on with I could always devote time to teaching an individual or a small group.

As well as the games and the workbooks, the rods and the practical activities, maths were often involved in our various projects. Once we were interested in the map of our own area, and from this developed an interest in buses and timetables. We drew a large-scale map for the wall with the distances between towns and villages marked; then we made a whole lot of bus tickets and the children worked out timetables and fares. This kept them busy for a long time and was much more fun than dull sums from a book.

On another occasion we were discussing the problems of measuring 'awkward shapes'; someone had wanted to measure a circle and had found the grid and square-counting method too inaccurate to satisfy her. So someone else suggested tracing the circle on to paper and then cutting it out, then folding it and cutting it into segments; she thought of the segments as triangles and was preparing to place them in pairs to form measureable rectangles, but at this point she saw the snag that the curved perimeter presented. To divert them from a problem that they did not yet have the means to solve, I produced a wooden sphere and asked them how they would measure this. The answers, from children ranging in age from five to eight, I thought were interesting.

One said: 'I would make a ball of Plasticine the same size, then squash it into a cube so that I could measure its volume'.

Another said: 'I would weigh it, then I would weigh cubes of wood too; I could find the volume of the cubes that weighed the same.'

A third child brought a straight-sided cannister, square in shape and made of transparent plastic, and said: 'I would put some water in this and mark the water-level, then I would push the ball under the water with my finger and mark the new water-level. Then I would find the volume of the cannister first up to the lower mark, then the upper mark, and take one away from the other.'

The others thought about this for a minute, then someone objected: 'What about your finger? If that was holding the ball down it would take up some room too.'

Silence for a moment, then the triumphant reply: 'All right, I would stick a needle into the ball and hold it just under the water with the very tip of the needle. That would hardly make any difference, would it?'

This answer satisfied everybody.

When we first began full-day school and were having lunch on the premises, we used to repair to the drawing-room for a rest after lunch. The floor was covered with a nice thick carpet and the children would stretch out on this and either take a short nap or look at books while I lolled in an arm-chair and drank coffee. Then I played records - they liked listening to music - and one day they were particularly fascinated by a Boccerini Flute Concerto that I had happened to put on. They knew enough now to be able to pick out individual instruments, and they loved that flute. We found a Mozart Flute Concerto too and played that - not the whole thing, just short flute passages - and in trying to explain to them about woodwind instruments I brought out the nearest thing I had in the house, a descant recorder. They all wanted to try it out, and the upshot was that everybody got recorders and Mrs Dyson was summoned to teach them to play. They were an amusing sight, as they played in woollen gloves because their fingers were still too small to cover the holes completely.

Mrs Dyson also taught most of them to play the piano, and although she had to leave us after a year or two they kept it up with other teachers. Deborah, Nicky, Sebbie, Isobel, Graham, and Michela are still playing the piano six years later; Nicky also plays a violin, Michela a guitar, Deborah a tenor recorder, and Jo is itching to get started on an oboe, furious because everyone says she is still too young. This is a problem which has dogged these children all along - the dogmatic assumption on the part of the adult world that their chronological age must decide what they are allowed to learn, regardless of their interest or ability. Deborah met the same attitude when she wanted to play the organ; she qualified in every way - that is, she had reached Grade five in piano - but because she was only eleven she was told patronisingly that she must wait another four or five years before she would be old enough to begin. Then people wonder why the young rebel!

It pleases me very much that the children caught their passion for music at an early age - if only more people could be introduced to music at an early enough age, many more would be able to share the new dimension of pleasure that music brings.

Mary and I were beginning to find the drawing-room too cramped for our more ambitious dancing sessions, so we took over a nearby church hall one afternoon a week. We still did a few singing games, though these were now the traditional English variety rather than the outgrown nursery ones. Most of the programme consisted of miming to music, free interpretation, or games to develop understanding of pitch, tone, and rhythm. We used to make up little stories, which the children would dance with great glee, involving the whole group - sort of miniature impromptu ballet.

To give an example - one favourite was a story of some mice who came creeping out of their holes after everyone was in bed to nibble crumbs on the kitchen floor; after a while the cat(s) began to prowl around, and eventually all the mice fled in alarm back to their holes, pursued by the cats. The children had to listen to the changes in the music to decide what stage the story had reached, and they soon began to listen much more attentively. The game of 'trains' was devised, among many others, to teach them to recognise 'time': here the children were divided into four trains, one of which ran in time to quaver beats, another walked to crotchets, another slow-marched to minims, and the last took only one stride to each semibreve. While Mary played something in four/four time I held up a card with one or other of the notes largely inscribed on it, and the corresponding train had to move in its own rhythm. We had many variations of this game, and eventually we dispensed with the cards and the children had to pick out their own rhythm by just listening to the music. Another game concentrated on pitch, alloting the low notes to the Bears, or the giants, or the elephants or whatever, and the high notes to the fairies or the mice.

We also did simple traditional dances like 'Sir Roger de Coverley', and when they were older Country dancing became very popular; then we made skirts out of old net curtains and decorated them with paper flowers for the girls, and stitched bells on to wrist- and ankle-bands for the boys, such as we had seen the local Morris dancers wear.

One period that I remember vividly was after we had been to see the Royal Ballet dance 'Swan Lake'. This made a very deep impression on all of them, including the boys, and for weeks afterwards, while Mary obligingly produced the appropriate music on the piano, they danced 'Swan Lake' again with a depth of feeling for the music and comprehension of the story that one would have said was impossible with children so young. Several of the girls went to classical ballet classes outside school, and they introduced a professional precision of movement that the others were quick to copy. More ballets were added to their repertoire as they saw 'Giselle', 'Coppelia', 'The Sleeping Beauty', 'Les Sylphides', 'La Boutique Fantasque', 'La Fille Mal Gardée'. When we had first taken the children to the matinee of the 'Nutcracker' the theatre had been half empty, but the following year the theatre manager had put on a special matinee for children and had circulated all the schools. Four years later it was almost impossible to get tickets - the theatre was packed out with school parties, and most of the children were under eleven. There was no doubt about the children's enjoyment of the ballet - if only more theatre managers were as enterprising as this there would be no need for Government subsidies for the arts in the next generation.

One rainy afternoon in February we decided that life was becoming humdrum. The weather did not encourage expeditions, and no one seemed to be having any bright ideas that might develop into an exciting new project.

'Let's have a Sale,' I suggested - we could always do with money for new equipment. The idea was taken up with enthusiasm and we immediately fell to discussing stalls, sideshows, and things to sell. I lugged my ancient sewing-machine to school, a hand-operated Singer of noble vintage better suited to the children's speed of operation than the modern runaway electric variety; we made plastic-lined cotton bags for carrying wet swimming-gear, more felt needle-books (found from previous experience to be a good line), tough denim children's aprons with animals appliquéd in check cotton, velvet pin-cushions to hang on the wrist, and lots of mobiles made of expanded polystyrene (for which we had a battery-operated cutter and a pile of left-over ceiling tiles). We had by this time become a little more proficient in woodwork - each child had made her own bench-hook, used primarily to protect the tables when we were cutting balsa wood with craft-knives; these had involved sawing, drilling, countersinking the screws, filling in the screw-holes, filing and sanding; so now we made use of the bench-hooks to make lots of wooden fishes, which after sanding and priming we painted gaily with enamel paint - a new technique for most of the children. A loop of wire was run through the nose of each fish, and a number painted on the back; fishing rods with hooks on the end of the line completed the equipment for a grander version of our old fishing game.

By this time my own family had moved out of the old house, so we had the large empty drawing-room to ourselves. Rebecca and Nicky, wearing old shirts of my husband's back to front, went to work on the Wendy House with pots of emulsion paint, giving it for a change blue wiggley vertical stripes on a white ground. Jose and Catherine ran up some new curtains for it on the machine, and Deborah and Candy painted a very fine signboard showing the Pickley Wizard head. Thus transformed, the Wendy House was set up in one corner as a café, where Rebecca and Nicky did a roaring trade in orange juice and biscuits.

Jose made vast quantities of fudge, fondants and other sweets, and set out her wares on the old kitchen table, tastefully draped with a rose-strewn paper tablecloth.

Deborah turned an old chest of drawers back to front, covered the back with black paper superimposed with dozens of white polystyrene elephants, and suspended one huge white elephant overhead; here she sold off everybody's unwanted pottery, jewellery, and everything else that did not seem to belong to anyone else's stall, as well as the things we had made in school.

Isobel had taken over the bookrack and was selling off all our outgrown books as well as those she had managed to beg from other families. Graham stocked the maths counter with everyone's spare toys - though he seemed to be having trouble with some of his younger customers who recognised their own possessions and demanded them back vociferously, while their mothers who had thankfully donated them tried to divert their attention. Candy and Clare sold children's clothes - we numbered some twenty children under ten in just our own families, let alone the visitors', and their stock would not have disgraced Marks and Spencers!

Downstairs Edward was dishing out presents from a bran-tub at threepence a go; Catherine was presiding over the bath-tub where people fished for the painted fish; and Sebbie and Elwyn were raking in all the gamblers' money on a cunningly contrived Hoop-la stall.

In the schoolroom Rachel ran a tea-and-recuperation service where exhausted and penniless parents collapsed when their offspring had finished with them.

Quite apart from the money it raised the Sale was an undoubted success. To begin with all our families and friends came, so it was a pleasant social event. The children had a lot of fun both in the preparation and in the event; they had learned much that was new to them in handwork; writing and spelling had been involved in the invitations and the notices, and even the youngest had helped to tot up the profits and were in no doubt about how to count in pounds, shillings, and pence. Moreover the dreary days of February and early March had sped unnoticed amid so much activity, and ahead lay Easter and the happy prospect of another summer term.

Parties were a regular feature of our school life. There were the numerous birthday parties throughout the year given by the parents; but the main, specifically school parties were at Hallowe'en and Christmas. The Hallowe'en parties began in the early days when some of the children went in great fear of black magic and I thought it would be a good thing to cut witches down to size. Also it proved to be a good time to have our own fireworks because a lot of the families had other commitments on Bonfire Night itself. So it became the practice early in October to make witch-hats, write out invitations, and go to the woods to collect twigs to make witch's besoms. The day before the party we would be busy hollowing out swedes for jack-o'-lanterns, painting jam jars to hold nightlights, and making sweets. Usually the party was held at school; all the parents and brothers and sisters came and we played games, bobbed for apples, ate sausages and toffee-apples and parkin. Outside in the light of the lanterns small witch-figures whooped and capered and performed their own ritual dances, and when they were exhausted sat in a circle to watch their fathers and elder brothers enthusiastically letting off fireworks.

The most memorable of these Hallowe'en parties happened one year when a farmer lent us his field for the occasion. A day or two beforehand an advance party went to gather wood and build a bonfire the size of a respectable funeral pyre. When the day arrived it had been raining, but determined Papas flung on quantities of petrol and ensured a good blaze. We slung lines of coloured paper lanterns between the trees, and some of the children carried lanterns on sticks like the Swiss children do. One family arrived with hot sausages, another with flasks of hot drinks, and in the glow from the fire the children contentedly sucked toffee-apples and fudge. Sparklers and golden-rains spurted and died in the darkness. Everybody had brought their fireworks - we had so many that the blissful fathers and brothers could have gone on through the night with a non-stop display, but eventually the youngest children began to droop and were borne home fast asleep on their parents' shoulders.

At Christmas we took over the church hall and had a fancy-dress party. The first time the mothers laboriously made the costumes, but this seemed like a lot of hard work, so after that it was the rule that the children made their own out of any props they could find at home or at school. There were prizes for the most effective, and some of their efforts were very amusing and ingenious: they certainly got a lot of fun out of it too. We numbered about fifty when we all got together, and these parties were a communal effort. One family would buy the prizes and take-home presents and wrap them up; another would arrive in the morning to decorate the hall with Christmas tree and greenery and clouds of balloons. Someone else made the Christmas cake, and others made mince pies and jellies. Like this the party just seemed to happen without undue effort on anybody's part.

Everybody came - fathers and mothers, big brothers and sisters, younger children and au pair girls, as well as all the people who had somehow got involved with us, and children who had been at the school for a short time in its early days. Everybody joined in dancing the 'Sir Roger de Coverley', young and old, long and short; it always delighted the children to see all their belongings involved in this ritual get-together.

It seemed a pity that Hallowe'en and Christmas came so close together. There were plenty of outings and picnics in the summer, but there seemed to be no excuse for a party between Christmas and Easter. Then the answer occurred to me - my own birthday fell in March; so to celebrate my fortieth birthday I invited all the children to a party. It was quite the nicest birthday party I ever had, and the children were charming guests. They were most impressed by the forty candles on the cake and gazed at me with a new deference to my great age (and, presumably, wisdom). We had a puppet show, and danced all round the house - in and out of all the rooms, up and down the stairs, and out into the garden.

Had I remembered the Easter hen I might have known that the children would not have forgotten by the next year. I had not mentioned 'the birthday' this time because I had something else on that evening and was planning to have the children's party a week or so later. However, the day before, one of the children remarked: 'It's your birthday tomorrow so we'll be having a party won't we?' All the children looked at me expectantly, so I thought fast and said:

'Of course, but it will be a lunch party this time, instead of a tea party. I shall take you all home with me after morning school, so don't forget to tell your mothers.'

As soon as school was over I rushed out to buy prizes and presents, and spent the evening cooking pounds of sausages, making gallons of ice-cream, and thinking up games to play in the garden. The next day Miss Wilson - who was one of the people who had got involved with us - helped me to ferry them all back to my house, and we all ate a satisfactory lunch of sausages, potato crisps, tomatoes and ice-cream, washed down with orange juice and Coca-cola; this was followed by a treasure hunt in the garden and games, and I sighed with relief that they had warned me just in time to do what was expected of me.

CHAPTER 7

The Final Year

We had always known that the life of the old schoolroom was limited; the house was due for demolition and redevelopment. I had imagined that as we ourselves would have to move anyway we would simply have to find a house big enough to accommodate the school too, or else put up a wooden building at the end of the garden. In the event it was just not as easy as that. The planning act passed somewhere around 1960 stipulates that there can be no change in the use of a building without specific planning permission, and that was just what nobody intended to give us.

Three times we found a suitable house, and asked the neighbours what they thought about having a dozen or so children around. Most of them welcomed the idea, thinking that it would solve their own educational problems, but each time one person objected, and this was enough to scupper us. One of the objectors was a man whose own teenage children nearly drove the neighbourhood mad with noisy motorbikes every evening; another woman objected on the grounds that one thing led to another, and that though she would not mind a few children, there might be a filling station there before you could turn round - an extraordinary line of reasoning, but I quote her words.

The only answer was to buy a building that was already in use as a school, but such buildings commanded a huge price because of their site value, and were much bigger than we wanted anyway.

In the end we had to buy a house for the family and look for separate premises for the school. With various parents I looked at endless parish halls and old barns, but none of them could be satisfactorily converted to our use. I was determined not to share a room with anybody else; we could have camped during the week in a parish hall that was used for meetings in the evenings and Sunday school at the week-ends, but it would have been impossible to achieve any sort of security and 'belonging' in this way; we must have a home of our own.

In desperation I went to one of the nearby Teacher Training Colleges to see if they could help. It had just occurred to me that they might welcome a group of real children on the premises to keep them in touch with the job! The man I saw however not only could not help, but was quite bitter that I should be wasting my time with these children. Why, he demanded, was I not teaching in a State school? I explained that I should not be allowed to do the sort of teaching I was doing in a State school as they are at present organised; besides I was having far more fun as I was, and I was determined to keep my children out of the system for as long as possible.

At the last minute we were saved by the generous offer of Isobel's parents of their dining-room - a big square room opening out on to a lovely old garden and playing-fields beyond. It was a great improvement on our old premises, and was so far from any neighbours that nobody could possibly object to our presence there.

By this time we were down to only nine children; Graham was eight and had gone on to his prep school; Michela's family had moved to Canada; and, the latest blow, Candy and Clare moved to another town. It was clear that we could not carry on much longer as things were. The whole venture was run on a non-profit-making basis, but with such a small number of children it was hardly paying its way. Moreover it was becoming rather too much for me physically - as well as a full-time teacher I was school cleaner, secretary, and business-manager; I also had a husband and four children to look after at home and no domestic help.

The only way out of the crisis was to expand into a 'proper' school, with something over a hundred pupils if it was to be economically viable. We would have to secure one of two school buildings in the town likely to come on the market at that time - which in itself would involve a great deal of political manœuvring, as I quickly discovered.

To find the hundred pupils did not apparently present much of a problem - there seemed to be plenty of backing from parents and teachers who would have welcomed this sort of school.

Money was more difficult, but the Pickley Wizard parents rallied nobly round, and we could probably have raised the capital we needed.

I myself was the stumbling block. It would have meant ten years of hard work getting such a school going, and though I would have loved the teaching, the business side would have bored me utterly. I knew that instead of pottering in the parks with the children, or teaching them to read, or just discussing with them whether Nelson was a hero or a conceited idiot, I should be running round after builders, making up to planning officials, organising appeals for money, and trying to find teachers who would teach the way I wanted them to instead of the traditional way. Maybe after all that the school would end up just the way most other schools are, so what would be the point?

In the end I decided to hang on as long as I could with the

nine children who were left, to keep them free just a little longer before they joined the herd. Nicky and Sebbie would be joining Graham at the prep school in another year, and Deborah too would have to take the entrance exam into the local high school if she was not to miss her chance for ever. But for one more year we could just enjoy ourselves, and we moved into the new schoolroom determined to make the most of it.

It was a beautiful room, perhaps thirty feet square with a high ceiling. The big curved bay window looked on to the garden, and along one side ran a conservatory with ample room for growing things - animal as well as vegetable - keeping coats and muddy shoes, and storing our vast amount of equipment.

The bay we screened off with the bookrack and a bookcase and turned into the reading corner, with Ooly and Jezebel perched on the windowsill. We pinned insulation board round the walls so that we could display our pictures and charts, and fixed our precious Bayeux tapestry over the fireplace. The maths counter fitted comfortably into one corner, and in another we established a music centre with the percussion instruments, dulcimer, music books, band charts, and a pretty painted table harp - this served to demonstrate the principle on which string instruments work but very little else, as it always went flat five minutes after we had spent twenty minutes carefully tuning it.

There was not really room for the Wendy House, but we had instead a permanent puppet theatre, complete with an assortment of puppets, for anyone who felt like experimenting with it. We still kept a shelf-full of toys for the younger members and for general relaxation.

I also had my indispensable blackboard and easel. I am told

that some education authorities have banned blackboards in primary schools, but how do the teachers live without them? I hauled mine around from group to group to demonstrate endless things that otherwise I should have to draw on bits of paper and pass round.

There was still plenty of room left for the red-topped tables with the gold stardust pattern - two sizes, to fit the large and the small - and ample space to walk round them or lie on the floor to paint. If we wanted to dance we could just push everything to the sides of the room and caper to our hearts' content.

The children particularly loved the garden. The seasons rolled by outside our own door and we did not even have to go as far as the park to watch the first buds uncurl. Some blackbirds nested in the ivy over the window and the children, by climbing up inside the room, could look right into the nest unobserved.

Now that there was a family in residence again to cope at week-ends, we felt that we might indulge in some new pets, so one afternoon we all trooped off to the market. We attracted some amused glances as we returned to school earnestly carrying a cage with a yellow budgerigar, and two cages each harbouring a baby hamster, plus all the impedimenta essential to their care. The bird was christened Lemon, and we hoped to teach her to talk. After our earlier experiences with the rabbits, the two hamsters, Fudge and Snowy, were strictly segregated. The cleaning and feeding of this trio added to our morning chores, but for a few months at least the children loved them and were interested to watch them at their antics. In the end only Nicky and Sebbie remained truly faithful, and eventually they took the hamsters home for keeps. Lemon never learned to talk, but when we were singing she competed in a high-pitched shriek worthy of the parrot house at London zoo; whether she was joining in or objecting we never discovered. She eventually went to spend her old age in Candy's care.

Ever since the children were quite small we had begun the day with a hymn, and later a prayer. The matter of religious education was a tricky one because several of the parents were agnostics, if not atheists, though others like myself were Christian.

Earlier we had a little Jewish boy who announced firmly: 'David is my King,' and claimed to have seen God looking in through the window - though when questioned, his description of the Almighty approximated so closely to that of his earthly father that we dismissed his vision as a purely psychological phenomenon. However, he went home to America before the era of morning prayers.

After considerable thought I decided to confine our religious activity to teaching the facts about Jesus Christ, the Bible, and the development of the Church, because in a Christian country this is a necessary part of understanding our own history and culture. I also explained briefly about the various denominations within the Church and where they differed from one another. I told them too about other religions in other parts of the world - Judaism, Buddhism, Mohammedanism, and so on, as well as touching on classical and nordic mythology and primitive tribal cults. I wanted them above all to realise how other people think, as a foundation to learning to think for themselves.

I do not myself subscribe to the practice of indoctrinating children from an early age with religion of any sort - or with anti-religion either for that matter - in the hope that they will accept the beliefs of their parents unquestioningly. It seems to me an unacceptable form of domination that seeks to prevent the child from making a truly free choice -

and is likely to fail anyway when he reaches the age of reaction from all that his parents stand for.

So, as in all else, we talked a lot about religion in our school, particularly about morality - albeit with reference to their fairly limited experience. If they found it difficult to obey the first great commandment to 'love the Lord thy God with all thy heart' because, as they said, how can you love someone that you can neither see nor hear? - there seemed to be more point in the second, to 'love thy neighbour as thyself.' When they really came to chew over the problems of living together, even in such a small community as ours, they realised that a true concern for each other was the only possible *modus vivendi*, unless life was going to be a pretty miserable affair for some, if not all, of us.

We discussed problems of behaviour that concerned us such as bullying, stealing, lying, teasing, bad temper (mine as well as theirs), intolerance and contempt of one another. We had to admit that all these things happened because we were human, but at least we recognised them for what they were, and thought about the effect of such behaviour on one another. Because we knew that we were all given to these faults at times there was less condemnation of offenders, and I think that such frank discussion, though it did not of course solve all our problems, lightened the atmosphere. It lessened the feelings of guilt with which children are sometimes burdened, and made bullying, either mental or physical, almost impossible.

For the rest, we observed the Christian festivals as they came round. At Christmas we sang the old carols and made a crib, told the Christmas story and discussed the implications of it. At Easter we made a little garden complete with the empty tomb, and tried to understand what the story meant to Christians.

On Ascension Day some of the children went off in the morning to beat the bounds of their parishes - an event which mystified the non-christians and made them green with envy, because the beaters returned laden with sweets and cakes showered on them by indulgent parishioners; one parish was in the centre of the town and they had to search out the boundary stones in some very strange places, such as the cellars under a shop, or in some city dignitary's garden.

The Harvest Festival, like Grace before meals, was a thanksgiving, as much pagan as christian, for the fact that we had enough to eat. I explained to the children how two-thirds of the world was not so lucky, because I thought it important that they should know this - maybe one day they will be sufficiently concerned to do something about it.

The Lord's Prayer, which we said every day, I still think is the best summary of what man can hope for from his God, whatever form God may take in his eyes. This I passed on to my children without compunction. This, and our Grace before meals, were our only prayers - and our Grace was simple and to the point, without reference to such irrelevancies as 'the birds that sing'.

The hymns we learned because they are as much part of our culture as our folk songs, and as such have very little to do with religion. We used 'Songs of Praise' because it seemed to have a larger number of good words and tunes than anything else we could find. Each child was given his own hymn book as soon as he was reading well enough to make use of it, so it became something of a status symbol. We also sang contemporary hymns - Sidney Carter's 'Lord of the Dance' was a great favourite, and we danced it gaily round the classroom with tambourines. Our favourite of all was what we called 'Grapes of Wrath' - better known as the 'Battle Song of the Republic'. We really let ourselves go with this one, using all the percussion we'd got and superimposing a soaring descant - the Salvation Army would have been proud of us.

To our great sorrow we had lost Mrs Hab a year or so before we moved - she was really an academic historian, not a primary school teacher, and she wanted to get on with work of her own. However she had already laid a sound musical foundation in most of the children; Edward and Antonia, who came later, could never quite fathom the (by now) instinctive awareness of the others. After she went I tried to carry on with teaching the children to sight-read music, and we did make some progress. It is not nearly as complicated as language-reading, and it should be possible to teach all children to read music as fluently as print if they are taught systematically. It is certainly an invaluable skill to possess.

Meanwhile I used my voice and the dulcimer to teach them more songs. We sang nearly every day - part-songs and rounds, ballads and jigs, with and without accompaniments.

Inevitably the church hall sessions changed. Without Mary at the piano the spontaneous ballet and the musical games were no longer possible. Various people tried helpfully to fill in, but we never again found anyone who could improvise well, and the stiff set pieces were better rendered on records. So we limited these sessions to the traditional English singing games of the sort collected by Cecil Sharp (plus some that we invented ourselves), and country dancing to records.

In the classroom, where we had our collection of musical instruments and our record-player, we danced and sang spontaneously, inventing our own accompaniment as we went along. Sometimes we preferred to put on a record and dance or mime to that, but we had no set time for these sessions, we just did it whenever the spirit moved us.

Miraculously, the gap left by Mary was filled in a way a little while later by Miss Wilson, whom I always suspected must have been drawn in our direction by telepathy. She was a music lecturer in one of the nearby Teacher Training Colleges, and her special interest was in teaching children to sing and *sight-read*. She was using the Ward method, which had been developed in France but was little known in England at that time, and she was looking for a pilot group on whom to try it out. I was delighted, needless to say, and from then until the close of the school she came twice a week to give twenty-minute lessons. I sat in on them so that I could consolidate her teaching on the days that she was not there.

The results she achieved were fantastic. Her enthusiasm was infectious, and she made the whole thing into a game that delighted the children. They were used to singing solo without embarrassment, but she developed their tone and voice production so that they sang accurately and roundly. Her method of teaching this was known as 'throwing balls'. She would announce that she was going to 'throw a ball' (in reality a note of a certain pitch) to a particular child, and the child must 'throw it back', in other words echo the note correctly. Sebbie, when thrown the ball, was once heard to remark 'Whoops! I've dropped it!' which everyone found extremely funny, but generally they entered into the spirit of the thing with enthusiasm. Gradually she persuaded them to read phrases in the tonic solfa, either from a diagram on the board, or even by holding up her hand and pointing a pattern on her fingers. From this they transferred to the stave, and soon came to understand bar-lines and time-signatures.

Another facet of the teaching concerned the construction of the tune itself. There was a game called 'tune-building' where one child would invent and sing the first phrase of a tune; the next child had to invent a suitable second phrase, the next a third, and the next a fourth and concluding phrase. Apart from the fact that they soon realised that you must not 'bring the tune back to Doh' unless you meant to finish it, this construction of melody was done entirely by ear - the theory came later. While the other children were singing, to the solfa names, another child would be detailed off to the blackboard to write the tune on the stave as it was sung. Apart from Edward and Antonia who had missed the first part of the course, they could all do this without difficulty, including Isobel and Rebecca who were only five, and Elwyn who was four. They could also of course sight-read any straightforward tune straight from the blackboard, so we did not have to learn songs laboriously by rote any more.

Miss Wilson was pleased but not surprised by the success of her teaching, but it seemed that she had some difficulty convincing her pupils and colleagues back at the College. So one day we all went along to take part in a demonstration lesson there. As a member of the audience of some fifty lecturers and students, I was amused to watch their scepticism change to amazement as the lesson proceeded. Elwyn nearly fell off her chair with amusement when one of her companions sang a wrong note, and was quick to point out the mistake. 'He sang "fa" instead of "me",' she chortled. Someone in the audience suspected that the children had practised the tune beforehand (they had in fact never seen it before), but were convinced when they heard them inventing their own tunes and writing them down as fast as they were sung.

One of the things that I particularly wanted to try teaching the children was French. I had experienced the abortive task of trying to hammer it into unwilling teenagers, so decided to try an entirely different approach. We began as soon as the children could read, write, and speak their own language fluently, that is somewhere between five and six. Most of them had been abroad and realised what 'speaking a different language' meant - which is an important point in itself. I once tried to begin teaching French to a class of eight-year-old boys who just could not understand what I was getting at; here was I trying to tell them that the thing I was pointing at was 'une maison' when they knew very well that it was a house, and no amount of my trying to explain seemed to get through to them.

So having talked a bit about France and the French, I produced a collection of twenty objects which could be handled and passed round - a ball, a pencil, a box, and so on; I also drew pictures of the twenty objects on a chart and made matching labels with the names. I explained that all nouns in French are masculine or feminine, and we learned the definite and indefinite articles so that we could talk about 'a ball' and 'the ball'. Then came a few phrases so that we could ask and answer questions about the twenty objects - 'where is the ball?' 'It is here', 'I've got it', 'Show me the ball', 'Give me the ball', and so on. The emphasis throughout was on talking, though the children learned to pick out the flash cards with the words and phrases printed on them; I never asked them to write French themselves.

Then we started on a children's French course, with a series of records and a corresponding picture book. The first part of the book introduced words that they already knew so they felt they were on familiar ground. Each child had his own set of records at home so that he could listen to them as often as he liked, and his own picture book which he brought to school each day for the twenty-minute lesson and took back home whenever he wanted to. Each day in school we listened to a short record, following first the pictures and then the printed transcription in the book. This way they acquired an accent which actually bore some relationship to the French spoken in France, unlike the anglo-saxon French that most English school children speak. The rest of the lesson was entirely devoted to talking, using the phrases we had learned in question and answer, and making up stories. Sometimes I would describe a picture that they would draw as I spoke, something like: 'I can see a house with four windows and a green door. There are pink flowers growing by the garden gate; and two children, a boy and a girl, are playing on the grass with a red ball,' and so on.

At other times we played games in French. The classroom would be turned into a restaurant where two children were waitresses and the rest customers. Another time it would be a toyshop, or a clothes shop, or a train with a family going on holiday. This way they were continually using the words and phrases they knew in natural situations.

Sometimes we played Lotto or Happy Families in French - we had various sets of cards for these games which increased their vocabulary enormously. Also I made sets of matching cards like those we used when learning to read, where you have to match the picture of an object to a card bearing its name.

The interesting thing was that, learning everything by ear and being untroubled by grammar, they would cope unconsciously with grammatical snares that had taken me years to sort out on the theoretical basis on which I had been taught. For instance, if you asked one of them how many eggs the hen had laid, he would reply 'il y en a dix' without hesitation and without any of the agonising about the order of 'en' and 'y' that had troubled my schooldays.

At the end of the year they could read very simple books in French, and could talk about ordinary everyday things, in the present tense at any rate. They would have coped much better than I did when at the age of eighteen, and after years of learning French at school, I was plunged into life in a large French family and could neither understand a word nor make myself understood.

My plan was to take as many as possible of them to France the following year to live among French children, at least for a few weeks. I wanted to take a house in France for the whole of one summer holiday and arrange for a French friend of mine, who taught English at a French school, to stay there too with an equal number of her children. It was complicated to arrange, however, and the school had to close before it happened.

One of the things that I felt was not a success at our school was drama. Though most of the children would mime to music with a complete lack of inhibition, and even act quite naturally in the French lessons, they were stilted and tongue-tied when it came to interpreting any dramatic situation in English. One or two of them overacted in their self-consciousness, others just giggled awkwardly and could not think of anything to say or do. I thought perhaps puppets would help - often the shyest of children will perform behind the anonymity of the puppet theatre. The puppets and the theatre were always available, and most of the children would pick up a puppet occasionally and try a few experimental movements with it. I kept out of this now because I wanted them to express themselves spontaneously, not just to copy me. Gradually two or three children would join together to produce a short show for the rest, but they never showed much originality - perhaps they were too young. To try and inject some new ideas I showed them different forms of puppetry - rod puppets, shadow puppets, marionettes, simple finger puppets - but these never caught on either.

Despite all this they were very anxious to 'do a play'. They had all been to see plays put on in the town by older children in a junior Drama club, and I think they longed for the glamour of the footlights. In the end I wrote a play for them, with a part designed for each of them, and told them that we would try practising it in the classroom, so that if it was any good we could do it for their parents. It was hopeless though - much though they wanted to do it, most of them just could not memorise the lines (or even make up their own as they went along), or act with any degree of naturalness, and in the end we agreed to scrap it.

There was no doubt that apart from their music and movement these children expressed themselves best on paper. Their imaginative writing and their poetry was impressive for five- to eight-year-olds. Their story-writing is lost - they always wanted to take it home with them to show their parents - but I do still have one book of poetry to which most of them contributed at some time or other. A few of these will serve to illustrate the variety of things they wrote about. The following were all written by five- and six-year-olds.

THE CAT NAMED GALLILLEE

The cat, he drinks his milk,
He has fur of silk,
You stroke, him, it's soft.
Cat sleeps in the hayloft.
He laps up all his tea,
But never in February
Because it is sour.
He goes to bed at a late hour,
This hour is in the morning.
He is mourning
For milk I see,
The cat named Galilee.

THE GHOST

Up from the dark
And rippling water,
Sitting in dreams;
Away it floats,
Away it floats,
Then goes back
To the dark and
Rippling water.

THE FUNNY GRASS SNAKE

There was once a funny grass snake
Who liked climbing trees.
He lived on other animals
Who swore they were not bees.
He lived in the long grass
And hunted in the reeds,
And caught all the animals
Who lived among the leaves.

THE MORNING FOG

You can see where the morning fog has been,
You can feel the cloud that shivers about you.
The morning comes over the houses,
You cannot see the end of the line;
You cannot see the balcony on the houses far away;
It is darker than a devil's shadow.

During that last year I was at pains to prepare the children for the formal maths that they would meet in other schools. We spent wretched hours learning to put figures into orderly columns and to draw straight lines, while the children moaned 'But why? I know what the answer is going to be - why all this boring writing?' I agreed with them absolutely - they could see that there are six twenty-fives in a hundred and fifty without the tedious business of writing it all out, and they could more easily tot up a shopping list with the aid of their own odd jottings than with the confusing ritual of columns and lines. This proved one of their greatest headaches at their new schools - they could solve the mathematical problems easily enough, but were utterly confused by the strange (and often to them illogical) methods of working that they were made to adopt. They found that they got into trouble for not putting the patterns of figures down properly, even though they arrived at the right answer, and this bewildered them - they had always assumed that what mattered in maths was understanding the problem and getting the right answer by any method that worked.

Apart from this, they had by the age of seven covered the ground that in the traditional maths syllabus was prescribed for the junior school up to the age of eleven; they had done a lot of interesting things too that come under the heading of 'New Maths' now, though at that time the first

Nuffield Project books had not been published. Their grounding in things like basic number bonds and tables was unshakable and stood them in good stead for ever afterwards. All this was not surprising because they had been spending a regular time on maths every day for years - they liked it, were interested, and could get on steadily at their own pace, without gaps, and without waiting for the slower ones to catch up. The process was always moving on to something new and interesting, but only after they had grasped the previous step to their own satisfaction; it never got boring through constant repetition of something already understood. The snag is that most of them found themselves way ahead of the class at their new schools and had to mark time for years, suffering agonies of boredom in the meantime.

The project work continued as before, except that their interest turned more and more towards 'how things work' rather than people. They were fascinated by electricity, and though they were too young to do much in this field I did bring a collection of magnets, wire, bulbs and batteries to school. We made compasses and electro-magnets, evolved lighting systems for dolls' houses and toy theatres, and made a lighthouse with a flashing light. We also made an electric bell, and a morse buzzer with which we sent each other messages.

Clocks were another subject of great interest, and we were lucky in finding a special exhibition on 'Time' mounted at one of the museums in the area. We studied with interest the progression of clocks from early sundials and Chinese water clocks to pendulums and the era of electronics. Back home we made hour-glasses and water clocks, marked candles with the hours, and tried to invent a mechanical alarm clock rather on the lines of Prof. Branestawm's efforts.

The garden made a great difference to our physical activities. The children had always walked a lot, swum regularly, and climbed like monkeys on their climbing frame and ropes and swings, but now for the first time they could concentrate on handling a ball well. We had a series of badges which were awarded for achieving a certain level of competence in a variety of fields; there were seven of these, for music, sewing, swimming, hand-writing, maths, nature study and gym, and for each one there was a test - to get the swimming badge you had to be able to swim a length of the swimming bath; for the maths badge you had to know all your number bonds and tables; and so on. For the gym badge you had to be able to throw, catch, and kick a ball reasonably well, skip with a rope, handle a racquet, and jump over a certain height. The children took a great interest in these badges and tried hard to get them - learning quite a lot of useful things on the way. When you had won all seven you also got a book token for £1, which was an added incentive.

If it had not been for our ever-decreasing numbers, I think we could have gone on learning and living together like this very happily for years. Sebbie and Nicky were beginning to feel the need for more male company, but the girls were perfectly happy. If we could have kept a dozen or fifteen girls together from the age of three until they were grown-up I think it would have worked, as long as we could keep on bringing people in from the outside to infuse new ideas, as Mrs Hab and Miss Wilson, and so many other people who became involved with us, had done. We would have needed too to be able to move about as freely as we had done in those early years - and farther afield as they got older.

The farthest we actually went was to Yorkshire, and that

trip arose out of a chance remark of one of the children. We were looking at some pictures of rolling fell country, and someone sighed and said: 'What a pity we don't have mountains like that in England!'

'But we do!' I exclaimed, thinking of the Lake District, the Derbyshire Peak country and the Yorkshire Moors. They were disbelieving; many of them had been abroad and seen marvels of scenery, but the part of England where they lived seemed to be one vast built-up area - it was certainly not the sort of place where you could walk for half a day without seeing a single cottage or a human being. So I promised to take them to the North of England.

Not all of them came - Antonia and Edward and Elwyn were too young, and the boys did not trust themselves so far from home yet, but in the end six of the girls came; Deborah and Candy, who were seven, Jose and Catherine who were six, and Isobel and Rebecca who were still only five but game for anything and determined not to miss the fun. We persuaded a young student teacher called Honor to come with us, and set off to York by train with our rucksacks on our backs.

We spent a few days in York, a city which enchanted the children. We explored the Minster and the narrow mediaeval streets; we spent a day at the Railway Museum, and two at the Castle Folk Museum - they would have stayed here for a week if we had had the time.

Then we went on to Richmond - a marvellous castle here to explore - and on up to Grinton and the moors. They had never seen country like this before and spent a blissful week tramping through the heather, exploring old lead mines, playing in the streams and climbing the hills. They got the feel of the village and the people and understood something of the life up there, with its emphasis on sheep and the woollen trade, so completely different from their own. Even the very plants and birds were different from those at home; they collected flowers and pressed them with their usual passion, and were delighted to find a species of bog-moss that even the teachers of a sixth-form, who were staying in the vicinity on an ecology course, failed to identify.

They grew brown and tough and independent in that week. They had to clean their own shoes and make their own beds, help with the washing-up and look after their own clothes. They walked miles, sometimes in the rain, and carrying their own luggage, and learned not to grumble when they were tired and uncomfortable. They afterwards maintained that it was their best holiday ever - something to do with the freedom, space, and fresh air, combined with each other's company.

On the way back we spent a night or two in York again because they found the place irresistible. One morning we were walking all round the city walls, gazing with interest into all the gardens and houses and backyards that our vantage point revealed to us. Here a gardener was tending a bonfire, there a family was having a belated breakfast; someone else was hanging out the washing. A cat was stalking a robin in an apple tree - we watched ready to warn the robin, but he was no fool; he let the cat crouch to spring, then flitted lightly to a higher branch out of reach.

'Look at that lovely old house,' remarked Candy suddenly. 'It would be perfect for our school!' We stopped and leaned on the wall to study the question. She was right - it would have been perfect. It was of soft grey stone with big white windows, and was surrounded by a green and peaceful walled garden, with tall old trees dotted here and there. We fell to discussing how, when they were all grown-up, we would run a school there together. 'A happy school, just like ours,' said Jo. Deborah would come and teach music, and Candy would tell them stories. Rebecca would paint and dance with the children all day, and Isobel would teach the little ones to read. Catherine wanted to read all her favourite books to the bigger ones, and Jo would teach them outdoor things like swimming. We were quite carried away by our dream.

'Look, we could put the climbing frame here, under these trees.'

'And we'll have to put a gate by the side of the house to stop the little ones getting on to the road.'

'It looks a nice big room behind those windows, and it must be beautifully light and sunny - let's have that for the main classroom.'

They thought then that our own happy school would go on for ever, that they would always be together, and that when they were grown-up they would simply take over my role and carry on the fun and peacefulness for other children.

I felt depressed and treacherous because I knew that soon they would all have to go away, and school would become a very different sort of place for them.

CHAPTER 8

So What?

Happiness - or as Joan Baez sings, 'with a satisfied mind'.

So what, after all, did the Pickley Wizard achieve? A few happy years perhaps, for a handful of children, and the beginnings of an education; though much of the detail of what they learned is now lost. I doubt whether any of them can still sight-read a tune, let alone invent one, and probably they have forgotten the French they learned to speak. Certainly for many of them the maths they knew has rusted through years of disuse, and they may no longer remember all their tables, though they have a basic understanding of number that will remain with them. Perhaps the most valuable thing they achieved was a love of reading, both for pleasure and as a means of widening their knowledge. They have retained their lively curiosity and interest in the world around them, and for this reason alone they still stand out in a crowd.

Quite apart from this however these children, after even a few years of this type of 'free' education, were quite different from any other group of children that I have ever taught. They had a positive attitude both to learning and to their environment that made other children seem negative; most children at that age absorb the world around them passively, but these children went out actively to claim it. They were confident and articulate, unafraid either of other people or of personal failure. Moreover they were already beginning to think for themselves, which together with literacy is the very essence of education.

The Pickley Wizard was not a scientific experiment - it was never meant to be; my object was simply to provide, for my own children and a handful of others, a happier and more worthwhile start to their school life than I believed they could have got at any other school I knew of. However my experience with these children convinces me that if you took a random sample of children from any part of the country, from any social background you like, and educated them from the age of three until they were grown up on the Pickley Wizard lines, they would develop into immeasurably happier, more stable, and mature adults than the children now being educated in the State schools.

The most important single factor in education is that children should be happy. Happy children tend to mature into healthy stable adults, an asset to any society; conversely, unhappy children tend to become emotionally sick and anti-social. A very large proportion of our children are still unhappy, or at least not nearly as happy as they could be, and are growing up frustrated and discontented, only half developed and with a genuine grievance against the 'system' for never really giving them a chance. They in turn are likely to become inadequate parents and so perpetuate their own unhappiness into the next generation.

The Pickley Wizard was an extension of the nuclear family, a small community of which each child was a loved and important member; it was this that enabled him to identify with the group instead of being threatened by it, to become an accepted part of society instead of against it. This is the very cornerstone of true education, if by education we mean fitting people to live happily and usefully in society. It is only in a small loving community that the child can learn to make successful personal relationships - a prerequisite of both personal happiness and social usefulness; for these must be rooted firmly in affection and respect.

Most children successfully learn their first lessons in community living at home. Naturally self-centred, they gradually learn that other people too have rights and needs and problems that have to be taken into consideration. Some children fail to learn the lesson at home either because they are spoilt - the family revolves round them simply because they are the youngest member - or, the other extreme, because they are completely dominated by the interests of the adults in the household and are themselves granted neither rights nor consideration. For either of these groups the lesson must be learnt in the wider world of school.

The school however must be a true community, where the rights and interests and opinions of the children are given equal weight with those of the staff. The old-fashioned sort of school where the children are completely subjected to the tyranny of the teachers is not likely to prepare the children to be responsible members of any society. It may dominate them, tame them to play their part as the docile unquestioning masses, or it may give them a bitter grudge against all authority; but if they are treated as unimportant individually, simply a commodity to be manipulated, they are unlikely to have any consideration for any other individual, or regard anyone else as important except in terms of victims to be exploited - either in school or in the wider world outside.

On the other hand, if in school at least the child is treated as an important individual, if his ideas and his opinions and his demands are taken seriously, he will then respond to the idea that the other children and the teachers are equally important, and he must treat them with the same consideration that he expects himself. This is the only way he will learn to have a proper concern for all other people - the compassion and understanding that we must all learn if we are to be a progressive society, and not just a mass of individuals each fighting against the rest for his own survival.

It is relevant that the particular children I taught all came from good professional homes, and were much loved by their parents - the latter a vital factor in the development of every child. No system of education can wholly overcome the effects of a bad home background, but a good school could offer the child a chance to grow up in a peaceful and healthy atmosphere that provided a valid alternative to an inadequate home. As things are school is no real alternative - too often the most wretched of the children bring the misery and sordidness of their home life into the school, and the school itself fights a losing battle against the values and mores of the children's background.

This is evident in schools at every social level. One immediately thinks of the deprived areas, where even though the majority of children may come from good homes, the few from a bad background taint the whole of the school life with their brutality, their vices, and their aggressive refusal to learn anything, so that none of the children have a chance to grow up sane and whole. The same thing can happen in a prosperous suburban school, where many of the children are imbued with the worst sort of middle class prejudices - snobbery, respectability, and a materialism which excludes any regard for humanitarian or spiritual values. Or again it can happen in the most expensive and exclusive private schools, which often contain a high proportion of unloved and neglected children, many from broken homes, and many more whose parents are too busy living their own gay social or professional lives to bother with bringing up their own children.

School could, and should, be a community so strong in its love and concern for each child that it can stand any amount of battering from the environment; a community strong and stable enough to absorb the deprived and unhappy children without being tainted by them.

I think that the particular development of the Pickley Wizard children was basically due to the fact that they were happy, at least as far as their individual temperaments allowed them to be at that age. Bearing in mind the conclusions I had formed as a child with regard to the elimination of fear and boredom, I deliberately arranged the day to day life of the school with the individual happiness of each child as the over-riding priority, taking precedence over accelerated development, academic success, or organisational convenience. This did not of course preclude order and routine, because I am convinced that these things are necessary for the happiness of everyone; but the order was liable to be disrupted by excitement and high spirits, and the routine was flexible. There was no punitive discipline, no regimentation; the children were free to come and go, to talk, to choose what they would do.

The old shibboleth 'discipline' probably causes more unhappiness than any other factor. I'm all for discipline - without it life is impossible for more than one person at a time - but a self-imposed discipline, not domination by one person over the group by means of threats and a lot of rules and regulations. Where the relationship between teacher and children is one of respect and affection, they work out an acceptable *modus vivendi* by common consent rather than by coercion. There is always the non-co-operative 'difficult' child in every class, but patience and understanding on the part of both the teacher and the other children are likely to be more effective than persecution. The child who makes trouble is always an unhappy or frustrated child, and needs more than anyone to be accepted and reassured. It is more to the point to try and diagnose the causes of misbehaviour than to punish the symptoms.

This relationship between the child and the adult world is important all through school life; if it was maintained consistently throughout, so that children were always part of a loving community, there would be no problems of discipline even in the difficult adolescent years. Certainly people as they change from children into adults yearn for more independence and claim the right to direct their own lives, but in a rational educational system they would not be continually frustrated in this. Moreover since they were already respected members of their own communities they would have no need to rebel against them because they felt rejected, as so many young people do now.

Competition as a learning incentive is allied to punitive discipline, and is equally unproductive. If a child is really interested in a subject he will learn as well and as fast as he is capable of learning, so that to compare his progress with that of other children is meaningless. Low marks serve only to discourage him and destroy his self-confidence, high marks encourage him to gloat over his companions and assume a false superiority. Each child's progress should be judged solely by his own standards, praise and criticism adjusted to the capacity of the individual. It is noticeable that the people who advocate competitive education are always the ones who came out on top themselves in such a system, though it is clear that academic competition does not necessarily select the best leaders for society.

Despite the lack of an imposed discipline, the Pickley

Wizard children were positively taught to live in a community. If they brought mud into the classroom on their shoes they were expected to sweep it up, which led them to be aware of the problem and make their own decisions about whether it was necessary to change their shoes when they came in from outside. They learned to put things away in the right place because they found it so infuriating when they themselves could not find what they wanted; to wash out paint brushes because they soon discovered that they were unusable the next day if they didn't.

They took a personal interest in the schoolroom and all the equipment because they felt it was theirs - they truly belonged there. If one of them left his Plasticine alligator on the windowsill he knew it would be there the next morning, because he had an equal right with everyone else to keep his things there. There were no hostile school cleaners to sweep his things away, no other classes would use the room. This was the essence of the children's security at school - which most schools fail to provide - and is the difference between spending your days in your own home, and 'camping' in a public place where you have no rights and no security of tenure.

This sense of 'belonging' is only possible in a small community. Once the group becomes too big for close personal contact the community becomes an institution, public rather than private, cold and impersonal. This is why schools at all stages should be split up into small self-contained units, inter-related as families in a village are inter-related, but where every child and teacher has his own 'place of belonging'. It is difficult to think of the traditional classroom, with its rows of desks, its inkstains and chalk dust, as 'home' in any sense; home implies order and comfort, a peaceful place to relax as well as work.

The old village schools had much of this sense of community, and this is why they fulfilled their function so much better than the vast and often inhuman town primary schools. I have never heard anyone who went to one of these small village schools speak of their schooldays there with anything but affection. The closure of the village schools is just one example of the priority given to organisational convenience over the interests of the children as human beings. These country children now have to travel into the towns by bus every day to attend schools which do not reflect their sort of environment at all. They were far better off in their old schools, and the cost of rebuilding or modernising these on their old village sites, in the midst of the children's own community, would be an infinitesimal part of the education budget as a whole - probably less in the long run than the cost of transporting the pupils into the towns.

In fact the town primary schools might well take a lesson from the old village schools and divide their children into small self-contained units with an age range of three or four years. These could still be grouped round the central facilities of the school to ensure that the plant was used to the best advantage.

A number of factors combined to make the early development of the Pickley Wizards different from that of other children. To begin with, their familiarity with me, with the other children, and with the pattern of our daily life together over a number of years meant that they could develop steadily and without interruption. This continuity seems to me to be of major importance. Normally children have to change schools between the nursery and the infant stage, and often again at the age of seven or eight - two or three different environments and different sets of teachers and children to get to know. Most children take about a term to overcome their shyness and feel really at ease in a new school, so each change represents a considerable check to progress.

One of the things that was so noticeable in the Pickley Wizard was the tremendous difference in the rate of development between the children who had been there since the age of three, and those who joined when they were older. The latecomers never entirely caught up, even allowing fully for a settling-in period. The training of the early years, from three to five, obviously had a dramatic effect on their development, but by the age of five it was too late to lay these foundations; by then basic learning attitudes were already formed, for good or bad, and there was very little that could be done to change them.

Self-confidence has a lot to do with personal independence and at our school this was deliberately fostered. From the age of two and a half the children were encouraged to do everything possible for themselves, from pouring out their own milk to lacing up their own shoes. From the moment he is born the child is engaged in a desperate struggle for independence, to master first his own body, then his immediate environment. The faster he can be helped to do this the happier he will be. It is more to the point to teach a small child to cope with his own clothes and feed himself than it is to do these things for him - even though the latter course may be quicker. The nursery school can help in this, especially when the parents are too lazy or too indulgent to train their children themselves. But the process is a continuing one; as the children grow older they have to be taught to cope with traffic, to keep their possessions in some sort of order, to keep themselves clean. Later they need to know what sort of food they need to keep themselves healthy, and how to cook it simply; to make and mend at least some of their clothes, and to wash them; to keep their living quarters clean; to cope with simple injury and illness. In coping with their environment they have to know how to make a telephone call, write a letter, look up a train, use a map. The earlier they can do all these things the greater their self-confidence; yet how many schools, or for that matter how many parents, ensure that their children get this fundamental education?

Physical confidence is necessary too - the control and balance needed to roller-skate, ride a bike, swim, handle a ball, climb. In any group of children at play there are always one or two who are nervous and hang back from the general rough and tumble - afraid of falling, of getting hurt, of not being able to keep up with the rest, of dropping the ball (the athletic children have no patience with their less agile companions). These children often go through life afraid of physical risk, and it can deprive them of a lot of pleasure. This is where an observant teacher could, with special attention and patience, help the child to overcome his fear at an early age - it is more difficult later.

One of the most deep-seated causes of unhappiness and dissatisfaction in people who live in the great conurbations is, I think, the rupture with any sort of natural life. An affinity with the earth and living things is instinctive in man since his earliest history - witness our tendency to grow things (pot plants if we have no gardens), to keep pets, to trek to the country whenever we get the chance. The denial of this natural desire is one of the greatest privations that the bricks-and-mortar children have to endure, and the schools must use every means in their power to compensate this lack.

Often the new schools have quite extensive grounds which could well provide a really wild garden - not with ornamental shrubs, and grass that no one is allowed to walk on, but one with real earth, trees to climb, bushes and trees to attract butterflies and birds, ivy with snails in it, nasturtiums with caterpillars on them, spring bulbs among the trees, flowers to pick, and space for the children to grow things themselves. There should be water too if possible - a little stream (even if it has to have a concrete bed) to paddle in and sail paper boats, a nice stagnant pond with weeds and dragonflies in summer, where you can fish for tadpoles - so much more interesting than staid goldfish.

If this is impossible, as it often is in the old schools in the centre of the towns, then the children should be taken two or three times a week to the nearest park; and if this is just a dreary stretch of muddy waste, or a prim place with 'Keep to the Path' notices, then the local council must be badgered to provide something better.

Better still, pile the children into a bus and ferry them to the real country. Let them wander there at will for half a day, absorbing the peace into their minds and lungs. Never mind trying to turn the expedition into a lesson with something to learn - let them just collect things, gather blackberries, light bonfires, fish for tiddlers, and discover the sort of things one does in the country; otherwise they may never discover their heritage, and always find the country boring and uninteresting.

Another thing which is worth mentioning here, and which contributed a lot to the peace of mind of the Pickley Wizards, was the firm anti-bullying policy. Where small children are thrown together there will always be bullying unless adults intervene to prevent it. We ensured against it in three ways: first there was always someone with the children when they were very small; secondly we took complaints seriously and never dismissed them as mere 'tale-bearing'; thirdly we taught the children in a very positive way that unkindness is wrong. It surprised me that so few teachers regard moral training of any sort as part of their job; they will teach the children faithfully to read and write, but leave them to find out by painful trial and error about the very fundamentals of human behaviour.

In our code unkindness was the major sin - the physical exercise of might over right, malicious teasing, the cattiness of which all girls are capable, ostracism of offenders, and all the other miseries which children traditionally inflict on each other. The more normally recognised sins of sloth, untruthfulness, even petty theft, came a lot farther down the list.

The elimination of fear in schools depends very much on the selection and training of teachers. Violence is on the increase in our society, and only teachers and parents dedicated to anti-violence are going to stamp it out in the next generation. This will not happen as long as teachers continue to assault children in school - investigation shows that, despite the law, a lot of petty bullying by teachers still goes on even in the primary schools - and as long as parents show themselves to be pro-violence in their attitudes. Violence is as implicit in racial and class hatred, in the rigid 'law-and-order' faction (who want to see people who threaten the existing social order hanged or shut away in prison), as it is in the disorderly gangs who throw bombs to get their own way.

All these things then ensure the happiness of small children - the security of a small loving community, a rational discipline, the continuity of a settled environment, the fostering of personal independence and physical self-confidence, contact with nature and freedom from bullying; but what of my second condition, the elimination of boredom?

The causes of boredom in school children are threefold: the

wrong subject matter, badly presented, with no regard for the child's natural concentration span.

The child wants to explore the world for himself and discover things in his own way. He cannot do this tied to a desk - he must be free to move about, to gaze at things, handle them, examine them at leisure. He must have time to spend on things that interest him and not be forever checked and frustrated by bells and timetables. Nor must his interests be confined within the narrow limits of a set syllabus. Of course time must be set aside for the learning of necessary skills, but these should be treated as what they are - only the means to an end; the end itself, the widening of the child's mind and knowledge, is infinitely more important.

The subject matter is wrong if it is forced on the child against his will. It is one thing for the teacher to offer a subject, but quite another to insist that the pupil memorises facts whether he is interested or not. Most people must recall the boredom of being made to draw diagrams of plants with all the separate parts carefully labelled; yet some of the Pickley Wizard children knew all about petals and stamens and leaf formation by the age of six, by dint of constantly looking up the wild flowers they had collected in order to identify them. In this case they wanted to know more about something that had caught their interest. There were other children who were not interested in flowers at all, and it would have been useless for me to have insisted that they too memorised the parts of a plant - even if by dint of much drudgery they had managed to do so, the information would have been meaningless for them and they would soon have forgotten it.

On the other hand a normal child is naturally curious and will learn avidly about things that interest him; in the same way he will learn mechanical skills, if he sees them as necessary to achieving his own goals. He will be eager to learn to read once he realises that this is the key to the enjoyment of books; he will want to write in order to express his own ideas; to compute so that he can spend his own pocket money, compare his height and weight with those of his friends, count up the marbles he has won. But all these skills must be for use in real situations, not theoretical ones invented by the teacher. A teacher is not only being a bore, but also missing a great teaching opportunity, if she makes the whole class write a composition about 'What I did in the Holidays', when one child is longing to write about how his big brother broke a leg playing football, and another has a marvellous idea for an adventure story, and yet another is full of excitement about his first trip on a hovercraft. Possibly half the class have nothing at that particular moment that they want to write about, and would be much better employed in reading, or trying to rig up an electric lighting system for a dolls' house, or composing music for a poem they have written.

The subject matter then is often wrong because it is teacher-oriented rather than child-oriented. Moreover the teaching method is often wrong too; the child learns best by experience, yet he is usually confronted with the teacher's verbosity, dull text-books, incomprehensible explanations. When direct experience is not possible, for instance, when learning about Australia, the next best way to learn is from visual aids (films, pictures) and discussion.

Fortunately talking is no longer listed as a major crime in most schools, though I still know quite a number of teachers who demand absolute silence from their pupils over unreasonably long periods. What adult would submit to such a rule! Even in the more enlightened schools however conversation and discussion are rarely encouraged for their own sake. Yet it is the best known method of communicating ideas and clarifying one's own understanding. Of course the teacher has always been allowed to talk - far too much sometimes; I have so often heard children say of a particular teacher: 'She's so boring! She just talks all the time - on and on and on!' Perhaps it would be more interesting to hear what the children have to say for a change.

The third cause of boredom is the disregard of the child's natural span of concentration. My own experience with very young children led me to believe that the ability to concentrate is largely a matter of training. The Pickley Wizard children were encouraged from the age of two and a half or three to work at a task steadily until it was completed. This was nothing to do with imposing a task on the child and sitting over him until it was done. The child chose his own task, and was given peace and time, free from other distractions, to complete it, thus forming a habit of concentration which had an enormous effect on his learning capacity and attitudes in later years. Bells and timetables, as well as the imposition of tasks by the teacher against the child's will, all undermine the child's natural powers of concentration. So does the system of teaching where the whole class is given the same piece of work, and the quicker children are made to sit silent and unoccupied waiting either for the teacher's attention or for the rest of the class to finish. This amounts to torture for an active child, besides being an utter waste of time and opportunity.

Learning through experience is not a new idea; most schools pay at least lip service to it, though all but a few remain at heart traditionalist in attitude. Some schools have experimented with it hesitantly, but made the mistake of supposing that the teacher no longer has any role in this child-oriented learning. This is of course not so, though the new role is considerably more demanding than the old one and a lot of teachers are afraid to take up the challenge, visualising disorderly mobs of children wasting their time and learning nothing. In fact the teacher must follow up and consolidate the children's work, because they have neither the staying power nor the overall knowledge to see a subject through on their own. The teacher must provide the relevant material and experience, the guiding hand, the encouragement, and the general direction of the project.

It must be very difficult to introduce free methods of learning to an older class who have been brought up on traditional lines, particularly with the impossibly large classes that so many teachers have to deal with; the more so because each teacher has the class for only one year, so that she has hardly trained them to respond to the free method before it is time for them to move on, perhaps this time to a teacher who is a rigid traditionalist. For this reason there must be co-ordination of method from the nursery school through primary, and right on through the secondary school as well, if the children are to get the maximum benefit from the new deal.

Apart from the general environment and the teaching method, two other factors marked out the Pickley Wizard from the rest - the structure of the groups, and the mobility.

Chronological age is known to have little to do with development, and various schools have experimented with vertical grouping - that is, grouping in one class children with an age spread of two or three years. What no one else seems to have tried is grouping by stages of development - and by this I mean all-round development, social and emotional as well as physical and academic.

At nursery and primary level children seem to fall into

four developmental groups: those who have not yet learned to live socially in a group; those who have, but have not yet learned to read; those who are actually learning to read and write; and those who have already mastered these skills and are ready to use them for enjoyment and the furtherance of knowledge. In a school structured on these lines all newcomers, of any age up to five or six, would start off in the first group. When it was felt that they had sufficiently accepted group life, had got over the tantrum stage, were toilet trained and reasonably co-operative, and had their aggressive instincts sufficiently under control for the other children's peace of mind, then they would move into the second group. Here they would go through all the play stages, both free and directed, that lead to the control of hand and eye and the perception of patterns needed for the mastery of reading and writing. When it was felt that they were truly ready for formal learning, and not before - no matter what their chronological age might be, nor how ambitious their parents - they would move into the third group, where everything was geared to the rapid and painless acquisition of the mechanical skills of reading and writing. Once these were mastered they would move on to the fourth group, where life would really begin. There would seem to be little point in subdividing this group except vertically, to reduce the numbers to manageable proportions. The process of learning is the same for every group after this - personal exploration, reading, absorption of what is read by writing and discussion, and by experience where possible. Obviously more mechanical skills can be added - musical skills, languages, mathematical expression and notation, use of artistic media - but these should be acquired quickly and excitingly, like the reading, for immediate use, not as though they had some intrinsic value.

There is always the problem of children who are unable to develop normally because of mental or emotional handicap. These children, once they become noticeably older than their group, should be put into special groups with the best teachers available to go at their own pace. Such groups would need to be smaller, to have priority on the equipment they needed, and in every way to follow the general policy of the school in developing each child as an individual to his own full potential.

To put these children in the regular groups seems to me wrong on all counts. They are overwhelmed by the greater ability of the other children, their own inadequacies emphasised, so that they cannot help but feel a failure. This leads either to passive endurance on the part of the less able child - a conviction that it is useless to make any effort at all - or to defiant trouble-making. Either way he is better off in a group where no one shines and his contribution is needed and useful. It is unreasonable too to expect the rest of the children to bear all the time the disruptive behaviour of their emotionally disturbed companions. When these children are together, however, a sort of group therapy often works, as it would not in a mixed group.

I am not advocating that these misfits should be totally segregated. For some activities they could be mixed with other groups, but they would always have their own sanctuary to retire to when life became too much for them. Moreover many of them would develop to the stage where they could take their place in the fourth group, and the wide age-range here would ensure that they did not feel out of place.

The other feature of the Pickley Wizard that set it apart from the rest was the mobility of the group. We spent a great deal of time outside the classroom, either pottering about the countryside, or visiting places of interest that threw extra light on our current project. This is where a lot of our learning took place; books and television are a good source of ideas and information, but a poor substitute for first-hand experience. Seeing, doing, sensing for oneself seems to me the only way of truly understanding anything; ideas and imagination must do duty where experience is impossible, but these only exist in the mind and because of this are only imperfectly understood.

This is why I believe that real education cannot take place just within the confines of the classroom. The annual trip to London plus one or two local outings that most schools provide are nothing like adequate. The classroom must be considered simply as a home base where the consolidation of learning takes place, but the real education must take place in the world itself. I do not believe that this poses an insuperable problem for schools. Considering the vast amount of money that is spent on buildings and equipment anyway, would it be so impossible for each school to be provided with its own bus and a driver who could double as caretaker or groundsman?

At the moment any attempt by a teacher to take her children out is foiled by miles of red tape. By the time she has got permission from the local education office, convinced the headmistress that the trip is really necessary, and accomplished the wholesale reorganisation of staff that the operation seems to require, the moment has passed and that particular interest has died.

The Plowden Report on Primary Education came out in 1966, and to read it one might imagine that the golden age had already arrived, in the primary schools at any rate. It is enlightened and humane, full of common sense and an individualistic approach to children's problems. It was published after the days of the Pickley Wizard, but in broad outline it advocates the same approach to education. Why then are there still vast numbers of children who hate school and who are not yet being truly educated there?

The first and most important point is that only a very few schools even approximate to the ideal school postulated in the Plowden Report. Many teachers, particularly the older ones entrenched in positions of power, remain deeply convinced of the superiority of the 'keep quiet, sit still, and do as you're told' method of teaching.

The second thing that militates against the new deal in education is the apparently insuperable problem of overcrowding and understaffing in primary schools. In actual fact this problem isn't insuperable at all - it just needs more money; more money for buildings, and more money to pay teachers and so attract more good people into the profession. Teaching is one of the lowest paid jobs in the country - you can earn far more in business or in a car factory - and a whole lot of people who would make excellent teachers just cannot afford to teach if they have a family to support.

The third point is that the present organisation of the school system makes it practically impossible to implement the spirit of the Plowden Report. As things are the system is geared to organisational convenience rather than the welfare of the individual child. Children are regarded as a commodity to be dealt with, like raw material to be processed, rather than as human beings. It is true that in a matter so complex as the education of millions of children there has to be overall planning and organisation, but within this it is possible to develop human cells geared to the needs of the individual. This is not only possible but vital, if the expensive new school buildings of which everyone is so proud are not to be mere prisons, where children pine for freedom to grow up in a natural environment, and suffer all the ills of their stunting confinement.

Not only the children but the teachers too are restricted by the rigidity of the system. As I discovered ruefully, in an ordinary school it is impossible to do the sort of teaching I did with the Pickley Wizard children. This is one alarming aspect of the suppression of private schools. In the past practically all the pioneering work in education, such as experimenting with new teaching methods and small classes, has been carried out by the private schools; the State schools were too hamstrung by a plethora of overlords - governors, local education authorities, and so on - to move in the vanguard of progress, though the work of the Nuffield Foundation is a sign of hope that this is changing. There are many good teachers who feel utterly frustrated because they are not allowed to teach as well and as fully as they are able - at every turn they come up against rules and policies, organisational and curriculum limitations, personal prejudice and political manœuvreing.

All this is not to underestimate the tremendous revolution that has already taken place, at least in our primary schools, in Britain during the last decade or so - a revolution that is regarded with wonder and admiration, not to say envy, in many other parts of the world. The trouble is, as in so many other forms of progress, that the technological solutions have outstripped the human ones.

CHAPTER 9

Why Go to School?

Enlightened as the Plowden Report is, it deals only with teaching method and organisation; I would go further, and question the whole purpose and content of education as we now accept it. If you can forget for a moment the traditional concept of education and consider what in fact children need in order to become happy, stable, mature and useful members of society, you will notice that at present we have all our priorities wrong.

Education is not to be confused with job training. The particular job one holds in the community does not much matter; society needs its farmers, garage mechanics, history teachers, as much as its administrators, garbage collectors, and hairdressers. This is where specialisation comes in, but it is only of secondary importance. It matters personally, in terms of money and social success; in one job you earn more money, so that somebody else gets less; you get a bigger slice of the communal cake so that somebody else has to make do with a smaller portion; you are overfed, and somebody else starves - or vice versa. It is this inequality in the social system that distorts the educational one too, but if we could get our educational priorities right so that we bred healthy and articulate members of society perhaps the rest of the mess would begin to sort itself out as a result.

Bearing in mind then that the happiness of the child is the first essential, what does he need to know in order to become a useful member of society? In the first place he has to be able to relate to the rest of the world, to get along with other people, to live in a community; and then to contribute to the human situation in a positive way. For this he must be both willing and able to find out what is going on in the world around him, to understand how other people think, what makes them tick - not just his own generation, but people in other age groups, in other social strata, both within and beyond his own immediate environment. He must be able to think for himself, make unbiased judgments, and then add his weight to the course of events and take responsibility for his own actions and decisions, to take a hand in shaping his own destiny. This ability to think for oneself is what distinguishes the educated from the masses - here I mean the truly educated, not merely those who have passed through the educational system; there are plenty of graduates who are incapable of an original thought. The masses as turned out by the present educational mill can be swayed by any glib speaker, witness agitators whipping up Union members in a factory yard, or the effectiveness of party political propaganda.

'The proper study of mankind is man' - though you might not think so if you took a look at what our children are learning in school. They seem to be learning a lot about what man has achieved in technological terms, but very little about what he is, how he behaves, how he thinks, what are his basic fears and needs, psychological as well as physical. And yet we must understand these things if we are to make sense of our world, with its frighteningly rapid change and the seething revolution which must engulf us all before long.

It is never too soon for children to learn about other people, and one of the best ways for them to do this is by discussion. If they are encouraged to notice other people, to talk about why they dress or behave or talk a certain way, they soon get the idea that people do differ widely from each other - in their circumstances, in their way of living, their opinions; and this is natural - not something to be afraid of or withdraw from, but something to find out about and to try and understand. For some reason schools have hitherto shied away from this problem. They have paid lip service to the study of man by concentrating on history and geography - that is, on the study of man safely removed by time or distance - but children are rarely confronted with the fact that the world that surrounds them is torn by conflicting interests and opinions. The object is presumably to lull them into a false sense of security, but I do not believe they are taken in by this; they are merely puzzled and uneasy.

Take the question of religion, which is glossed over with a formal nod to the God of the Christians which deceives nobody and is almost worse than nothing. Children come to school with half-baked prejudices and cant-phrases gleaned from their parents, for or against this or that faith, which they use as battle cries against the other camp - down with the godless, or the Catholics, or the Jews. Yet if we aim at educating them, at revealing to them the world in all its diversity, we should tell them about all the principle faiths and creeds, and teach them to respect every man's beliefs and opinions.

We should try to explain too, without bias, the political beliefs held sincerely by different people - communism and socialism as well as fascism and conservatism; what the Establishment stands for, and what the revolutionary movements are about. As they get older their libraries should contain works about all the world's great leaders, not just those extolling the virtues of the British empire and the current ruling party. It is more important, for instance, for them to know about Gandhi and Karl Marx than about Henry VIII and Disraeli.

The most important way for them to sort their ideas out is to talk about them; so having listened to their teacher and read their books, they must be free to argue, to quote friends' and parents' opinions. They must get used to the idea of listening to other people as well as persuading them, modifying their own views as they learn, reasoning things out for themselves and forming their own opinion. Above all they must learn that books and teachers do not necessarily tell the truth, that this is something they must assess for themselves.

What about the time-honoured subjects on the primary school syllabus, the history, geography, scripture, and so on? Of course they have their place, as part of the study of man, but a lot of the detail in which they are taught is unnecessary. Young children are always fascinated to know how people live in other parts of the world, what other countries look like, what they grow and make there, and why, what the weather is like, and so on. But they don't need to memorise the name of every mountain and lake, the population of every town, or be able to draw maps from memory - all these things can be looked up when they are needed. Better by far to stock the library with good reference books and teach the children to use them than try to turn the children themselves into walking encyclopaedias.

The soul-destroying passion for stuffing children full of useless facts and then trying to make them memorise them belongs more to the secondary school than to the primary now, and with luck it will one day be discredited altogether; but there are still many primary teachers who stubbornly insist on delivering a 'lesson' to their hapless class, making the children learn it and write it until they 'know' it, and then administer tests to make sure that they can remember it. This is not education - it is mere memory training.

If an important part of education is the study of man, an equally important part is the discovery of the material world - the natural and applied sciences, which have less than their share of attention on the syllabus. Everybody, not just the few who are selected for training as scientists and technologists, has a right to know how his television works, how his house is built, how his clothes are made. Only the most academic minds can cull these things from books, but everybody can understand if he is part of a group that is making a television set under expert guidance, works even briefly on a building site, tries spinning and dyeing and weaving his own piece of cloth, cutting and sewing a garment. Such knowledge is likely to be of more practical value than the subjects usually taught under the heading of science, such as the digestive system of a frog, what happens when you combine certain chemical substances, or the angle at which a beam of light passes through a glass prism - all right for specialists perhaps, but hardly relevant to everyday life.

Once we have sorted out what we mean by true education, there remains the urgent question of how it is to be organised; and this seems to me to raise two crucial issues. In the first place, is the present school system the right one in moral terms - have we any right to force school on unwilling children and parents? Secondly, is it practicable? Can we afford it in purely financial terms?

It seems to me one of the greatest oppressions of our society that we force children to spend all their childhood years, when they should be happy and free in a way that they cannot be once they are grown up, imprisoned in the highly unsatisfactory schools of the present day. The only possible justification for such oppression is that it is inevitable, that they are happier in school than they would be at home, and that they learn more there than they would if they were left to their own devices.

To take the first point first - are the children happy in school? I am convinced that the majority of children, if asked, would prefer not to go to school, but to be free either to wander around discovering the world for themselves or to join in the work of the adult world at their own level. No doubt I shall be howled down by large numbers of teachers and parents who will swear that their children are idyllically happy at school, but the only way to find the true answer is to ask the children themselves, which I have been doing for years. If you ask a lot of different sorts of children whether they like school, the response will fall into two distinct categories: the clever children who happen also to be at a good school (that is, one where the staff are both kind and good at their job, and are more interested in the children than in the organisation of the school), will tell you that they love it, most of the time. The rest, the not-so-bright that make up nine tenths of the population, and those at the bad schools, will look at you as though you are mad even to ask such a question. Their reaction varies from apathy to bitter loathing, but they all long for the time when they will have served their sentence and can escape into the adult world.

The second possible justification for compulsory school is that children learn more there than they would if they stayed at home. It is true that most children would not learn to read and write if they stayed at home, though for children from professional homes this does not necessarily apply; many of them can and do learn without the help of the schools. Literacy is however of vital importance; but this, as I pointed out earlier, can be taught much more quickly and painlessly than it is at present, and would require the child to attend school for perhaps only an hour or two each day. Moreover the present system only begins the process of literacy - a very high percentage of school leavers are unable to read for either pleasure or information; the most they can do is to read notices and the captions under pictures - very few adults read informative books.

The only things I learned at school before the age of fourteen were reading and writing, elementary computation, and a love of the Arthurian legends - all learned under the two good teachers I came across in the very few months that I ever enjoyed school. Once I could read and write I would have learned 'English' anyway because I read and wrote extensively at home, and had access to more books than I could read at the municipal library. All the rest - the French, German, and Latin, General Science, History, Geography, and Scripture - were a complete waste of time; despite untold hours of drudgery I had to learn all these things from scratch after the age of fourteen. Maths alone was any use as a foundation for later work, and the ground I had covered in those early years could quickly and easily have been made up later.

We are told that education is a matter of developing the child's full potential. I am convinced that my full potential would have been better developed almost anywhere than imprisoned in those ghastly schools. Perhaps if all my teachers had been of the calibre of Mother Catherine and Katie Northern I should be telling a different tale, but all I was left with was a fine collection of nightmares and inhibitions, and a fear of adults that I had hardly overcome by the age of thirty.

If this was only my problem it would be unpardonable of me to bore everyone with a long exposition of my childhood troubles, but the fact is that this story could be told with but slight variations by a good percentage of the population, including the children who are at school now.

One important factor in children's happiness and development is the company of other children. When you talk to them about school this is the main reason they give for wanting to be there at all. In present day society if they stayed at home most of them would be truly isolated, each shut up with his mother and siblings in his own little concrete box. It would be different in the country perhaps, or in a simpler society where the children could potter safely in the gardens or among the houses without danger from fast traffic or machinery, where there were always people around to keep an eye on them, and nobody was quite so tense or so busy; but in a modern flat or housing estate both mother and children would be driven to distraction.

Because of the break-up of old community patterns and the isolation of nuclear families there is no longer any place in the community for children. They have to be herded together to keep them off the dangerous streets and out of the way of adults who are too busy to look after them. In an ideal world, where adults were kinder and more patient, I think children would be happiest going to school for just a short time each day to learn to read and write, and spending the rest of the time, at least until they were old enough for job-training, with adults, learning about the world from them in natural work and living situations, discussing things with them, and reading. They would grow up as an integral part of the community, respected as such, instead of in isolation.

The fact remains that in the 'civilised' world nobody wants to be bothered with the young - the more sophisticated the society the less it wants its children. In our own moneyed classes parents send their children away to boarding school; in America the people who can afford it tend more and more to get rid of their children even in the holidays by sending them to summer camps. In primitive societies children are luckier, and on all the evidence much happier. People who have lived among Eskimos, or among simple African or South American tribes, tell of children who play happily in and around the villages, never shouted at or smacked by neurotic parents, but accepted and loved by the whole community.

It seems then that in our over-civilised society school must function as a highly expensive baby-sitting service; but if the children must go to school, let us at least make sure that they are happy there. This is possible, but it needs a quite new relationship between children and adults, and a complete reassessment of the function of schools.

The other vital question is whether we can afford the sort of education that I have outlined for our children. The answer is clearly 'no' if we think in terms of the existing system. Astronomically rising costs are bound to mean less and less money for all public services - fewer teachers, fewer buildings, less equipment. There is a limit to expansion, and we are already very close to it. Unless we change our concept of schools this is bound to mean progressively poorer education for our children in human terms - machines and television instead of teachers, mass lectures instead of small groups, dehumanisation on a massive scale. As with so many aspects of modern living, from the big cities to the health service, the educational system is breaking down because the problems have become too vast; it can only cope by processing people in an inhuman way, and this is having such a deleterious effect on the human beings involved that the very fabric of society is tearing apart under the strain.

More and more people are realising that the problems of modern society have to be solved at grassroot level, and education is no exception. The education of our children is fundamental to the sort of society we want, the sort of lives we want to live; it is thus very much our concern as parents and as local communities. By abrogating this responsibility to a professional élite we are selling out our children's future, allowing them to be manipulated by an outside authority over whom we have no control. It is not enough to say that we elect our government at both national and local level, and must therefore leave these bodies to tell us what is good for our children. Many of the people on local education committees and governing bodies are quite unfit to direct the education of anybody's children.

Recently a friend was telling me of his anger and frustration when he went to register his son at school for the first time - and I think his experience is typical. The headmistress refused to show him over the school - there would be an opportunity for this, she assured him, during the school holidays for all the new parents at once; this way the parents never saw the school during working hours. He asked whether there was a parent-teacher association, and was told wryly that there was indeed, and that the staff had a job to stop it interfering in school affairs. He felt that he had to hand his son over to these strangers without any means of knowing whether the child would be kindly treated, let alone well taught, and yet he had no choice. He could not afford the fees for a private school - in any case he was already paying taxes for the education of his children. However good or bad the school - and he had no means of knowing which - he was forced by law to submit his child to it; he had no rights in the situation.

This is ridiculous! It is an intolerable oppression of both parents and children – so why do we, the parents, put up with it? It is our money that pays for the schools, they belong to us, the community. So why should we submit to being excluded from everything that goes on in them - and by the very teachers whom we are paying, at that! It doesn't make sense, and yet we all accept the situation docilely, and let our children suffer because we are too lazy or too cowardly or too unconcerned to do anything about it.

The crux of the matter, the factor which is really militating against the interests of the children, is the mutual antagonism and distrust that exists between the teaching profession and the parents - and speaking as one with a foot in either camp, I think the chief blame for this lies with the teachers. The people who run the schools (and the administrators are equally guilty here) feel that the education of the children is exclusively their business, nothing whatever to do with the parents - while I maintain that everything pertaining to the child, his happiness and particularly his education, is very much the concern of his parents, and that they have every right to ensure the one and direct the other.

Teachers maintain that they could not possibly cope if the school was overrun by parents - which is true in a way, if you visualise the teacher's job as exercising a precarious control over a wild and dangerous mob; but I find something very sinister in this. Why do our children, who are rational human beings at home, become so difficult to manage in school? There is no doubt that they do; but there is something wrong here. Can it be that they are under such strain at school that it causes them to behave abnormally?

Somehow schools must be freed from the stranglehold of professionalism and opened to the local community, to whom they rightly belong. Teachers must serve, not dominate; their training after all is in teaching skills - they hold no prerogative on education itself. The school doors must be flung wide open to allow a two-way traffic - pupils going out into the community to learn, and the rest of the people coming in to teach, to help, and (why not?) to learn alongside their children.

Such a school would serve as a focus for a new sort of community life, solving at the same time many problems of modern living. To begin with, it could banish the isolation of the nuclear family. There would always be work for willing hands, and company for lonely people of any age - preparing meals, helping in the nursery, painting classrooms and other maintenance jobs, making equipment, teaching special skills like football or photography. Adequate canteen and crèche facilities could liberate mothers hitherto housebound with young children.

To some extent such a project could be self-supporting, releasing available funds for capital equipment that could not be made locally, and wages for full-time teachers and organisers. One could visualise workshops for making the school's equipment; market gardens producing some of the food for the canteen; adventure playgrounds, even small buildings and swimming pool, constructed with the help of local builders. Needless to add that the children would work alongside the adults in all these tasks.

It would involve a lot of voluntary labour, but would have the effect of uniting the neighbourhood in a common purpose, the results of which could be enjoyed by everybody. It might solve that perennial problem, the school leavers - what better service project than working for the benefit of your own community.

This would only work if the local people had a real stake in the venture. The school board must consist of people who are genuinely involved in the daily life of the school, not the local bigwigs. School staff would be appointed (and sacked if necessary) directly by the board, who would also be autonomous in directing the general policy within the school. Safeguards could be built in to prevent a takeover by a particular faction.

The people who helped to run the school would also have to enjoy its facilities, from the swimming pool, canteen, and workshops, to the freedom to attend classes and the school cinema. This way the plant would be used for the benefit of the whole community.

The changes I am advocating will not come about without a struggle. People who have power never give it up if they can help it, and education authorities are no exception. On the other hand there are many teachers who would support such change wholeheartedly; large numbers of people within the profession are just as frustrated and oppressed by the present system as are so many of the children and parents.

Any worthwhile improvement in life involves a lot of work for a lot of people - patient conscientisation[1] of the people concerned, organisation of pressure groups, tireless insistence on the right of people to direct their own lives. But if just one community could persuade their local authority

[1] I make no apology for using this word, borrowed from Paulo Freire, because it has no synonym. It means 'making people aware of the facts and implications of a situation'.

to let them run their own school and prove what could be done, I believe it would only be a matter of time before the whole country followed their lead.

This is an ideal to be worked for, but it will never be achieved by bureaucratic means. It must be a living thing created by people for themselves, and for their children; it will only happen if we, the parents and the teachers, are sufficiently concerned for our children to make it happen.